D1265767

WHAT SORT OF HUMAN NATURE?

MEDIEVAL PHILOSOPHY AND THE SYSTEMATICS OF CHRISTOLOGY

The Aquinas Lecture, 1999

WHAT SORT OF HUMAN NATURE?

MEDIEVAL PHILOSOPHY AND THE

SYSTEMATICS OF CHRISTOLOGY

Under the auspices of the
Wisconsin-Alpha Chapter of Phi Sigma Tau

by

MARILYN MCCORD ADAMS

MARQUETTE
UNIVERSITY
PRESS

Library of Congress Cataloging-in-Publication Data

Adams, Marilyn McCord.
    What sort of human nature? : medieval philosophy and
the systematics of christology / by Marilyn McCord Adams.
        p. cm. — (The Aquinas lecture ; 1999)
    "Under the auspices of the Wisconsin-Alpha chapter of Phi
Sigma Tau."
    Includes bibliographical references.
    ISBN 0-87462-166-6
    1. Jesus Christ—Humanity—History of doctrines—
Middle Ages, 600-1500. 2. Philosophy and religion—
History. 3. Philosophy, Medieval. I. Title. II. Series.
    BT218 .A27 1999
    232'.8—dc21
                                                99-6523

© 1999 Marquette University Press
Printed in the United States of America

MARQUETTE UNIVERSITY PRESS
MILWAUKEE

The Association of Jesuit University Presses

Prefatory

The Wisconsin-Alpha Chapter of Phi Sigma Tau, the International Honor Society for Philosophy at Marquette University, each year invite a scholar to deliver a lecture in honor of St. Thomas Aquinas.

The 1999 Aquinas Lecture, *What Sort of Human Nature? Medieval Philosophy and the Systematics of Christology*, was delivered on Sunday, April 25, 1999, in Room 001 of Cudahy Hall, by Marilyn McCord Adams, the Horace Tracy Pitkin Professor of Historical Theology, at the Yale Divinity School.

After her undergraduate education at the University of Illinois, Professor Adams earned a Ph.D. in philosophy in 1967 from Cornell University and became professor of philosophy at the University of California, Los Angeles, where for twenty-one years she taught medieval philosophy and philosophy of religion. During this time she also earned two Masters in Theology, in 1984 and 1985, from Princeton Theological Seminary, was ordained a priest in the Episcopal Church in 1986, and served in various parishes in the Los Angeles area.

She has held fellowships from the Guggenheim Foundation (1989-90), the American Council of Learned Societies (1989-90), and the National Endowment for the Humanities (1974-75).

Professor Adams's distinguished record of publications includes, besides translations and edited works, her two-volume study, *William Ockham* (1987), and her book, *Horrendous Evils and the Good-*

ness of God forthcoming from Cornel University Press.

Among her many articles, chapters in books, and articles for encyclopedias, some of the most recent titles include: "Ockham on Final Causality: Muddying the Waters," *Franciscan Studies* (1998); "Final Causality and Explanation in Scotus' De Primo Principio" in *Nature in Medieval European Thought* (1998); "Reviving Philosophical Theology: Some Medieval Models," in *Miscellanea Mediaevalia* (1998); "Chalcedonian Christology: A Christian Solution to the Problem of Evil," in *Philosophy and Theological Discourse* (1997); "Scotus and Ockham on the Connection of the Virtues," in *John Duns Scotus: Metaphysics and Ethics* (1996); "Satisfying Mercy: Anselm's Cur Deus Homo Reconsidered," *Modern Schoolman* (1995); "Duns Scotus on the Will as Rational Potency," in *Via Scoti: Methodologica ad mentem Joannis Duns Scoti* (1995); "Praying the Proslogion," in *The Rationality of Belief and the Plurality of Faith* (1995); and "Memory and Intuition: A Focal Debate in Fourteenth Century Cognitive Psychology: Introduction, Edition, and Translation of Scotus' *Ordinatio* IV, d. 45, q.3," *Franciscan Studies* 53 (1993).

To Professor Adams' distinguished list of publications, Phi Sigma Tau is pleased to add: *What Sort of Human Nature? Medieval Philosophy and the Systematics of Christology.*

What Sort of Human Nature?

Medieval Philosophy and the Systematics of Christology[1]

I. Introduction

In 451 CE, the Council of Chalcedon issued its "two-natures/one person" definition, which set the boundaries for medieval Christology within the Latin West. The promulgation spoke of

> ...one and the same Christ, Son, Lord, Only-begotten, recognized in two natures, without confusion, without change, without division, without separation; the distinction of natures being in no way annulled by the union, but rather the characteristics of each nature being preserved and coming together to form one person and subsistence, not as parted or separated into two persons, but one and the same Son and Only-begotten God the Word, Lord Jesus Christ; even as the prophets from the earliest times spoke of him, and our Lord Jesus Christ himself taught us, and the creed of the Fathers has handed down to us.

Philosophical theologians clarified: 'person' in this context does not mean a center of thought and choice but—after Boethius—an individual substance; in the hands of schoolmen, more precisely the *supposit* of a rational nature. Normally, each supposit has one and only one substance nature and each individual substance nature one and only one supposit. God is metaphysically remarkable in that—among other things—the absolutely simple and singular Divine essence is supposited by three persons, and the Divine Word (i.e., God the Son, the second person of the Trinity) supposits two natures—the Divine essence necessarily and an individual human nature contingently. Chalcedon set itself against "Nestorian" approaches that seemed merely to place Divine and human natures side by side without any real union between them. Chalcedon also determined against various attempts to "hybridize" Divine and human natures in God the Son, insisting that each retains its natural integrity, altogether unmixed and unconfused. In particular, Chalcedon insisted that Christ's human nature included a *human soul* as well as a human body. The Council of Constantinople in 680 CE drew out the consequences of this assertion, affirming that in Christ there are two centers of consciousness and *two wills*.

Yet, such conciliar pronouncements scarcely exhaust the topic of Christ's human nature. For Peter Lombard notes what patristic discussions had already postulated—how human nature has found itself in a variety of conditions, corresponding to the different stages of salvation history: *ante-lapsum*, after the fall but before grace, after the fall but under grace, and glory.[2] What sort of human nature did Christ assume? One like Adam's and Eve's before the fatal apple? One fallen and ungraced like murderous Cain's? A human nature such as ours, fallen but helped by grace? A human nature already glorified— impassible, immortal, capable of walking through doors or ascending through unriven heavens? If each of these states is compatible with as well as accidental to human nature, Christ could be fully human in any one of them. Patristic authors had already begun to debate the question, what was Christ's human nature like during His *ante-mortem* career?

Like the "Chalcedonian definition" itself, answers to this question are a matter of speculative interpretation. On this issue, the Bible is neither silent nor prolix. More to the point, it is neither fully explicit nor systematic. Consequently, it is not self-evident how to integrate its various testimonies into a developed account of the sort of human nature Christ assumed. The task of weighing and balancing will appeal not only to *"ex professo"* comments, but to a broader range of Biblical and conciliar themes— among others, to those that furnish an appreciation of Divine Goodness, Wisdom, and Power.

My hypothesis in this paper is that conclusions about Christ's human nature are *systematically driven*, and vary principally with a theologian's estimates of the purposes and proprieties of the Incarnation on the one hand and of the multiple and contrasting job-descriptions for Christ's saving work on the other. Secondarily, focus of detail and choice of style in the portrait painted are markedly affected by the

pallet of philosophical tastes and commitments. In
what follows, I will test this estimate against a sam-
pler of six influential theologians (Anselm, Peter
Lombard, Bonaventure, Aquinas, Scotus, and
Luther). My effort will be to split out which theological and philosophical motives are correlated with
what features assigned to Christ's human nature. My
aim is to be, not only historically informative, but
also constructively suggestive. My hope is that analyzing the views of others will make us more explicitly aware of the issues that underlie our own intuitions and form the foundations for our own points
of view.

II. Anselmian Minimalism:
Soteriological Necessities

The obvious place for a medievalist to begin is
with St. Anselm's *Cur Deus homo*.

2.1. The Improprieties of Incarnation

Recall how in this polemical work, he tries to demonstrate the conditional necessity of the Incarnation and passion of Christ to "infidels" (probably to
Jews and Moslems, who accept the existence of God
and the authority of Scripture) who argue against it
from the metaphysical aloofness, the Justice, and the
Wisdom of God. Wisdom would deem it irrational, indecent for a being a greater than which cannot be conceived to degrade itself on the ontologi-
cal scale. Likewise, Wisdom dictates elegant simplicity, economy: why would God endure the humiliation of becoming human and suffering death

on the cross, when Omnipotent Kindness could liberate sinners by *fiat*? Justice forbids making the innocent suffer for the guilty. Consequently, the passion of God's obedient only-begotten Son could only make matters worse.

Anselm ingeniously stands "infidel" objections on their heads. Using the metaphysical "size-gap" between God and creatures to measure the seriousness of sin, and insisting that above all God must be just to Godself, Anselm contends that only the undeserved death of a God-man would suffice for satisfaction.

Important for our present purpose is the fact that Anselm seems to concede that Incarnation is a drastic step. Even though he stresses that the Divine nature is in no way altered or diminished by its assumption of an additional nature, taking a finite and temporary "almost-nothing" human nature into the unity of person is still something Divine wisdom and good taste would avoid, other things being equal. Consequently, Anselm tries to minimalize the metaphysical degradation involved, maintaining that the God-man's human nature has only those limitations that are necessary to accomplish His saving work, which Anselm sums up in three tasks. The principal one, on which the main argument of *Cur Deus homo* turns, is that of making satisfaction for the sin of Adam's race. The second is reversing the devil's conquest of Adam's race by conquering the devil in turn.[3] The third is the pedagogical work of teaching human beings by word and deed how to chart the course of this present life.[4] Anselm insists that

[t]he assumption of a human nature into unity
of a divine person will be done only wisely by
Supreme Wisdom. And so Supreme Wisdom
will not assume into its human nature what is
not useful ...to the work which this man is going
to do...[5]

2.2. The Exigencies of Satisfaction

According to Anselm, for Adam's race to be re-
stored to its original dignity, it is not enough for the
Divine Word to assume some human nature or other.
Rather the Divine Word must take its human nature from and thereby become a member of *Adam's*
race. Otherwise Adam's family would be "beholden"
to a "middle-man" (its benefactor) rather than to
God alone.[6] Moreover, Anselm adds, it is obviously
more fitting if this human nature is taken from one
rather than two parents—to parallel Eve's non-sexual
creation from virgin Adam, more fitting to be taken
non-sexually from a virgin; because Eve was taken
from a male alone, a fitting reversal for Christ's human nature to be taken from woman alone.[7] Likewise, to make satisfaction for sin, Christ must render to God in His human nature what Adam's race
always owed: throughout His human life spontane-
ously to uphold justice for its own sake. For humans were given the power of reason to discern
goods, to discriminate goods from evils, the better
from the lesser; and then to will accordingly. God is
the Supreme Good. Therefore, Adam's race owed it
to God to make love of God above all, and for His
own sake, and hence total conformity to His will, a
spontaneous offering. But this will be impossible if

the human nature Christ takes from Adam's race bears the taint of original sin, which includes lack of affection for justice, the obligation to have it, a weakened body, and a weakened soul. For without the *affection for justice* the human soul could not will anything under the aspect and for the sake of justice. Again, if He were born in original sin, He would be *personally* liable to make satisfaction and not merely a member of a family that owes the debt. Consequently, Anselm denies that Christ's human nature was affected by original sin.

To render God what Adam's race always owed, Christ's *actual* obedience to the Divine will must be total. Were He not *sinless*, He would—once again—owe His own personal debt of satisfaction to God.[8] Further, Anselm insists, nothing in His job-description requires Him to be capable of sinning; consequently, the human nature of Christ is *impeccable*: Christ can sin if He wills, but He cannot will to do so.[9] Anselm seems to hold that Christ's Divine will causes His human will always to uphold justice for its own sake. Such obedience still qualifies as self-determined and spontaneous, however, because of the hypostatic union: it is *Christ's own* Divine will that controls *His own* human will.

Again, Anselm insists, ignorance would be counter-productive to the human natural function: Christ needs to be *omniscient*, not just in His Divine but also in His human nature, in order for His human soul to love all goods and discern goods from evils perfectly. Following some patristic sources, Anselm insists Christ did what Adam was meant to do—exercise this function throughout His human life—and so He enjoyed life-long omniscience, even if He did not manifest this to others during infancy and childhood.[10]

To make satisfaction for sin, Christ must also render to God something He didn't already owe (otherwise, there would be no surplus to pay off the family debt). What could this be but suffering and death? Anselm argues that humans are not by nature mortal—death neither is, nor contributes to that for which God made human beings.[11] Consequently, the obligation to die is not something Adam's race acquires via its obligation to be and to do that for which human beings were made.[12] Following Augustine, Anselm insists that the necessity of dying is a punishment—a frustration of human flourishing—imposed for sin. Thus, Anselm reckons that death is something that human beings would not owe to God insofar as they remained innocent. Accordingly, obedience *unto death* could constitute the "surplus" offering that Christ could make on behalf of Adam's race. To this Anselm adds an argument from reversal:

> is it not fitting that man, who by sinning so stole himself from God that he cannot remove himself to any greater extent, should by making satisfaction so give himself to God that he cannot give himself to any greater extent?[13]

Anselm concludes that to make satisfaction, the God-man must *be able* to die with respect to His human nature. Yet, to die, to permit Himself to be killed, to lay down His life and take it up again, or not, always remains within His control as omnipotent Divine Word.[14] By the same token, propriety of reversing the pleasure of sin through the suffering distress of the passion makes it fitting for the Divine Word to assume, not an impassible human nature, but one capable of *suffering*.[15]

2.3. Other Job-Requirements

Christ's roles as teacher and conqueror of the devil likewise carry implications for Christ's human nature. Reversal dictates that if the human race was conquered with ease, Christ's human nature should conquer with difficulty—in this case by suffering unto death for the honor of God.[16] Again, Anselm declares, Christ the Teacher "should be like us but without sin" in order to teach us not simply by word but by example. Thus, He should be able to suffer pain and insults, the better to show us how to bear up under them. Would it not help were Christ to share others of our weaknesses: ignorance, the ability to sin, unhappiness resulting from suffering? Anselm insists not. If Christ were ignorant in anything, this would undermine His credibility with respect to everything else.[17] Again, Christ does not experience *our unhappiness* in addition to pain and suffering, because unhappiness involves experiencing something unwillingly or with compulsion, but Christ experiences whatever pains, etc., voluntarily and without compulsion from anything outside *Himself*.[18] Anselm seems to think that neither actual sin nor the ability to sin is relevant for pedagogy, because what Christ is supposed to furnish is an example of upright living.

Notice, Anselm does not understand it as part of Christ's job to *empathize* with us in our sin and suffering. His *identification* with us is *metaphysical* (by taking on a human nature) and *biological* (by becoming a descendent of Adam). His identification with us is *for legal purposes*—to make satisfaction without being a middle-man. Christ's purpose in suffering is not for Him to experience what it is like for us, but rather to enable us to identify with Him as a model and mentor of how to pass through our suffering.

2.4. Summary

Anselm's characterization of Christ's human nature is driven both by philosophical and soteriological considerations. From his point of view, it is metaphysically mind-boggling that God became human at all, and it would be easy to go too far in making Christ's human nature like ours. As to similarities, Christ's human nature includes "all of the essentials": both body and soul. Like ours, Christ's human nature is taken from Adam's race. Like ours, it is capable of suffering and death. Like us, that man owes it to God to be and to do that for which humans were made. As to differences, Christ's human nature was created without "taint" of original sin, and so—like Adam's—was created with the *affectio iustitiae*, without any personal obligation to make satisfaction, and free from any weakness of body or soul. Unlike ours, Christ's human soul was omniscient from the beginning of its existence. Unlike us, Christ's human will was unable to will to sin; unlike us, the Divine will's exercise of control over the human will did not rob Christ's human willing of spontaneity. Unlike us, Christ's person was in full control of whether or not His human nature would die or rise. Unlike ours, Christ's suffering in His human nature was voluntary and so did not make Him unhappy in His human nature.

If Anselm's formulation of the satisfaction theory of the atonement became classic, his characterization of Christ's human nature coincides with a mainstream of patristic conclusions and leaves some issues unexamined. For example, Anselm seems not to worry about how a human soul—"almost-nothing," creature that it is—could have infinite cognitive capacity. He does not develop the idea that omniscience would include knowledge of God. Nor does his human psychology furnish resources for any extensive explanation of how voluntariness would be sufficient to turn pain and suffering into a happy experience. Moreover, Anselm's focus is so narrowly systematic that while he is respectful of Scripture, he does not pause extensively to weigh its testimony regarding the characteristics of Christ's human nature, nor does he elaborate the philosophical ramifications of these claims.

III. Lombard's *Sentences:* Shaping Tradition

Equally seminal for later Christology, but in a different way, was Peter Lombard's *Sentences*, a syllabus of four books of the most important theological questions, focussed by citations of authorities— texts of Scripture, Church fathers, occasionally philosophers—organized into *pro* and *contra* arguments on either side of an issue. Lombard concentrates on "setting up" the problems and sketching a course that takes account of most or all of his citations rather than on an extensive development of his own view. Because commenting on the *Sentences* became a thirteenth and fourteenth century degree requirement for doctors of theology, Lombard's selection of questions and authorities as well as his proto-answers shaped Christological discussions by the great school theologians.

Lombard recognizes that our question—what sort of human nature?—is non-trivial. His criteria take the form of two further questions: what is fitting for Him? what is expedient for us?[19] Lombard's general reply is that because Christ came to save all, it is fitting for Him to assume a feature from each of the four states through which human nature passes: immunity from sin, from our *ante-lapsum* condition; punishment and other defects that accompany human nature after sin and before grace; fullness of grace from our present dispensation; and inability to sin (*non posse peccare*) and contemplation of God from the glory to come.[20] When it comes to advantages that Christ's human nature enjoys over our present condition, Lombard reasons to their propriety from Scriptural comments and patristic opinions, from the hypostatic union of that human nature with the Divine Word, and from various soteriological job-descriptions. Extravagant claims are checked by alternative passages and by philosophical estimates of the finite capacities of created human nature. The defects Christ shares are expedient for us, but limited by other job-requirements as well as by the perfections that are fitting for Him.

3.1. The Advantages of Hypostatic Union and Headship
(1) Impeccability?

The tradition within which Lombard worked was already convinced that the Divine Word would not assume just any kind of human nature. Anselm was clear that the Divine Word would not run the risk of His own human nature's sinning. Lombard considers an argument that makes the dangers explicit: "if He could sin, He could be damned and so not be God, because He cannot be God and simultaneously will iniquity."[21] Lombard replies with a distinction. Obviously, the *person* could not sin and could not fail to be God, because the Divine Word is God necessarily and eternally. But the human *nature* is united to the Divine Word contingently. Lombard contends, if it existed without being united to the Divine Word, it could sin as much as any other human nature could.[22] At the same time, he rejects as "frivolous" the inference (attributed to Abelard) that since Christ's human nature has free choice, it can sin even when hypostatically united to the Divine Word. Without explaining how, he reasons *a fortiori*, that if the blessed angels have free choice and yet are so confirmed in grace that they cannot sin, so too the human nature assumed by the Divine Word![23]

Assuming its compatibility with freedom, impeccability over-reaches but at the same time guarantees *the sinlessness* necessary for other dimensions of

Christ's saving work. For the Bible advertises Christ [i] as *conqueror of the devil*[24] *and of sin*[25]; [ii] *as the One Who takes our punishment*—every temporal penalty owed for sin—on the cross[26]; and [iii] as the One Who *merits our redemption* by perfect obedience, not simply unto death on the cross[27], but from conception.[28] And it is resolute innocence that conquers sin and the devil, perfect innocence that allows all His suffering be for the sake of Adam's race, continual innocence from birth that allows His entire life to earn merit.

(2) Fullness of Grace

If Christ is the One "in Whom the fullness of Divinity dwelt bodily" (Colossians 2:9) and "to Whom the Spirit was given without measure" (John 3:34), the One ever at the Father's side from Whose "fullness we have all received grace in place of grace" (John 1:16), would His human nature not be full of wisdom and grace (Luke 2:40)? If His role as Head of the Church and fontal source of all grace would not require fullness of grace *from conception*, would not the fact of hypostatic union with the Divine Word make this fitting?[29] Yet, Luke 2:52 reads, "Jesus *grew* in wisdom and age (*aetas*) and favor (*gratia*) with God and humans."[30] Likewise, Ambrose takes this Scripture to imply "that Christ grew according to His human sense" and so did not know everything—did not even recognize father and mother—in infancy.[31]

Lombard's resolution follows the patristic majority report: that qua human and from His human beginning, Christ received such fullness of wisdom and grace that God could not confer any more on Him—indeed, He could not become a human that lacked fulness of virtue and grace[32]—but (explaining away Luke 2:52) there was a growing manifestation of and expansion of benefits to others of His wisdom and grace.[33]

(3) Scope of Wisdom and Knowledge

Would it not be fitting for Christ's human nature to have wisdom equal to God's and to know everything that God knows? For Walter Mortagne, the main reason to the contrary is the metaphysical "size-gap" between Divine and created natures: "the Creator's equal is not found in any creature"; rather "God" must be "greater than creatures in any and every respect."[34] Yet, Scriptures tell in favor: for "the Spirit of God Who alone scrutinizes everything" (I Cor 2:10-11) was given to Christ without measure (John 3:34); and Colossians 2:3 identifies Christ as the One "in Whom all the treasures of Wisdom and knowledge are hidden."

Once again, Lombard charts a *via media*: the *scope* of Christ's human knowledge matches the Divine, but the created act by which it knows will not be so metaphysically worthy or furnish the maximal *clarity* of knowledge found in the Divine essence.[35] Even so, it will enable the soul of Christ to contemplate each creature clearly and as present[36] and will include a contemplation of God as well.[37]

(4) The Limits of Human Power

Does Luke 1:32—"He will be great and will be called the Son of the Most High?"—imply that

Christ's human nature will be omnipotent as well as omniscient? Ambrose seems to say so. Lombard begs to differ, distinguishing between omniscience which the human soul of Christ was naturally capable of having, and omnipotence—the capacity for doing whatever God does or can do—which exceeds the capacity of any created nature.[38] Still, Lombard recognizes a sense in which the human nature was to receive such power: viz., that it was to be hypostatically united to the Divine Word that eternally possesses such power.[39]

3.2. Expedient Defects!

Do such fullness of grace and the perfections of knowledge and impeccability that characterize Christ's human nature from its beginning mean that it is always fully glorified, in the way it was after the resurrection? Obviously not, it would seem. Doesn't the Bible testify to His death as crucial to the drama through which He conquered sin and the devil,[40] took our punishment,[41] and merited our redemption? Surely His crucifixion presupposes a passible, mortal flesh.[42] Likewise, doesn't Scripture bear witness to a passibility of soul, which bears our griefs and sorrows (Isaiah 53:4), is "sorrowful unto death" (Matthew 26:38), which is disturbed (John 12:27) and fears to drink the bitter cup (Luke 19:41; Matthew 27:35)?

In fact, Lombard records how patristic discomfort with the notion that Christ experienced any real sorrow (*dolor*) or passion spawned some creative interpretations. For example, Augustine insists that Psalm 22:3—"I cried out, but you did not answer"—

applies not to Christ the Head, but only to His Body the Church. And Jerome dares "them" to "blush who think the Savior feared death and said 'Let this cup pass from me' out of fear."[43]

Once again, Lombard threads his way through the maze of conflicting citations with his needle-like maxim, "Christ assumes all our defects except for sin—[all those defects] whose assumption was fitting for Him and expedient for us!"[44] A passible human nature *was* expedient, not only for the above-mentioned reasons, but also because it advertises *the reality* of the Incarnation: the passible mortal flesh demonstrates that He had a real as opposed to a phantom body; the passible soul[45] subject to real emotions (e.g., *dolor, tristitia*, and fear) shows He had a real soul.[46] Humans thereby convinced are rescued from despair, encouraged by the evidence that even passible, mortal human nature can rise from the dead and enter into eternal life.[47]

Lombard emphasizes that Christ as sinless did not assume our *guilt*[48] and so did not *merit* to have a passible human nature,[49] and so was not subject to its changes *necessarily*, but *voluntarily* and for our sakes.[50] Explaining away patristic citations to the contrary, Lombard suggests they meant to deny, not *the reality* of fear and sorrow (*tristitia*), but any *necessity* of His suffering them for His own personal sins.[51] Likewise, personal demerit did not make it necessary for Christ to suffer and die, but He voluntarily assumed a human nature that would suffer and die when whipped, punctured by nails, etc.[52]

Lombard distinguishes not only Divine and human wills in Christ, but also rational (*affectus*

rationis) and sensory affections (*affectus sensualitas*)
in the human will. Christ's perfect sinlessness means
that His rational affection always wills whatever the
Divine will wills (e.g., to suffer and to die), but His
sensory affection moves against them (e.g., refusing
to suffer and to die as in Mark 14:35—"Father, let
this cup pass from me").[53] Christ does not take on
the ignorance and difficulty that are consequences
of Adam's fall,[54] so that flesh strives against the Spirit
and against God.[55] Rather Christ's emotions are
more *propassiones* than passions, in the sense that
these feelings can never move His human soul from
uprightness or distract Him from the contemplation of God.[56] Apparently, Lombard takes it for
granted that Christ does not need to be visibly overcome with emotion or lose sight of the Divine presence, in order to save us, who frequently experience
these things, from despairing of a remedy for our
condition.

IV. Bonaventure's Reflections

In his *Sentence*-commentary, Bonaventure—then
a university man and future Minister General of the
Franciscan Order—offers us a Christology that is
already strung out in the polar tensions that struc-
ture his later spiritual writings, between Christ's
cosmic and redemptive roles.

4.1. Incarnation Anyway?

For Anselm, the Incarnation is a drastic move that
God would have avoided had it not been necessary
to accomplish His purposes in the face of human

sin. If many of his successors hesitated to say that the Incarnation was *necessary* in the sense that Divine power could not have achieved Its purpose another way, they nevertheless identified the remedy of sin as the *principal* reason for the Incarnation, however many other benefits might be integrated into it. In the end, Bonaventure agrees.[57] But first he pauses to weigh the arguments of some earlier thirteenth century thinkers—most notably, Robert Grosseteste—who begged to differ, contending that God would have become Incarnate even if the human race had not fallen.[58] These latter argue that even apart from human sin, the Incarnation would have been an eminent manifestation of Divine Goodness, Wisdom, and Power.[59] For the Incarnation would still have made for the perfection of the human race and hence of the whole universe, by completing the human race with respect to nature, grace, and glory.[60]

(1) First, the Incarnation perfects human being *with respect to nature,* because it completes the four possible ways of producing humans (from neither male nor female; from a male alone; from male and female together; from female alone), and because it joins the beginning (the Divine Word as creative source) with the end (human nature as last created) to form a circle, the most excellent shape![61] Again, it wouldn't be fitting for the creation of the noblest creature—viz., the soul of Christ—or the actualization of human nature's noblest capacity—viz., that for hypostatic union with a Divine person—to be only for the instrumental purpose of redeeming sinners.[62] Likewise, it would seem contrary to justice

for human being to gain the highest dignity of Incarnation as a consequence of its own malice towards God![63]

(2) Second, the Incarnation perfects human being *with respect to grace.* For the Anselmian metaphysical gap between Godhead and human being
makes it just as impossible for sinless but finite souls
to reach infinite goodness by their own power, as it
is for any mere creature to make satisfaction for sin.
For even apart from sin, nothing finite can do or be
anything intrinsically or essentially worthy of union
with God. Therefore, even apart from human sin,
the Incarnation would be worthwhile to enable us
to earn merit through Christ, Who is immeasur-
ably worthy.[64] Similarly, apart from the Incarnation,
Christ's Body would be headless. For the head of a
body is "conformed to" (of the same species as) its
members, and the source that directs their move-
ment and enlivens the senses. But it is in the Incarnation that Christ becomes conformed to human
beings, and the source of their charity, grace, and
perfection.[65]

(3) Third, the Incarnation perfects human being
with respect to glory. For glory perfects the whole
human being—the body, the senses, the intellect.
Just as the Divine Word gives the mind's eye something to see, so the glorified assumed human nature
gives the bodily eye something to look at, so that
the blessed human "passes over" into God with both
corporeal and spiritual parts.[66] Thus, if benefits for
humankind are what overcome the Anselmian presumption against the Incarnation created by the
metaphysical "size-gap," so also and all the more so

should be such perfecting of humankind apart from sin!

Bonaventure feels the force of these arguments. Insofar as the conclusion—that Christ would have become Incarnate even apart from human sin—is based on considerations of excellence and order, Bonaventure deems it more in accordance with "the judgment of reason." Bonaventure declares both positions to be defensible, recognizes each to be held by devout Catholics, and acknowledges how both in different ways stir the soul to piety.[67] Bonaventure finds it difficult to say which of these is the truer. Nevertheless, he thinks it more consonant with piety to regard the Incarnation chiefly as a remedy for sin. This is the only reason mentioned by the authorities (Scripture and the Saints). It *inflames* the faithful more to think of the Incarnation as cleansing them from pollution than abstractly to consider how it perfects the universe. And it commends the mystery of the Incarnation to emphasize how placating God and restoring everything after sin would require something drastic.[68] Again, speaking of the Incarnation as perfecting the created universe seems to subsume God under the rubric of perfecting God's works. Bonaventure finds it more respectful to see hypostatic union as surplus goodness, over and above what may be required for the completion of any created being; likewise, more pious, to regard God as transcending every created order.[69] Even if the capacity for hypostatic union contributes to the dignity of human nature, it does not have to be actualized for humans to be the noblest of creatures.[70]

Of all the many benefits of Incarnation, Anselm's polemical strategy seizes on satisfaction for sin as the one that makes it necessary. So also Bonaventure denies that Incarnation would be necessary for *gracing* humankind. Apart from the fall, the human mind would not have been darkened by sin, and would have been able to read the Book of Nature; God's power, wisdom, and liberality would have been so obvious in creation that there would have been no need for God to meet humans at the level of their sensory attention in the Incarnation.[71] Likewise, the merit-gap could have been bridged by sending the Holy Spirit into our hearts, without sending the Son of God into the flesh.[72] Nor—Bonaventure thinks—is Incarnation necessary for *glorifying* the blessed in heaven. Surely it would be more pious to say that seeing the Divine nature would be sufficient to beatify the whole, the glory of the superior parts (e.g., intellect and will) overflowing into the lower (sensory and bodily) parts![73]

4.2. Deformity as a Requirement for Union with God

If Bonaventure thus identifies remedy for sin as the chief reason for the Incarnation, considerations of excellence are ever before his mind as he allows his portrait of human nature to be governed in the first instance by the cornerstone thesis of his spirituality: viz., *that union with God presupposes deformity.*[74]

(1) Sensitivity to the metaphysical "size-gap" between God and creatures makes this maxim far from obvious. Anselm's objectors insisted that it would

unfitting to the point of blasphemy for God to unite Godself to any created nature at all. Bonaventure's objectors reason that because any created nature is infinitely distant from the Divine, there would be no more reason for God to join Himself to one created nature rather than another.[75] Bonaventure follows Augustine and Anselm, however, in balancing an appreciation of the "size-gap" with the recognition that all created natures are just ways of imperfectly imitating God, and with the acknowledgement that imperfect imitation comes in degrees, generating an excellence hierarchy. Natures that lack life, sense, or reason are mere vestiges that are incapable of *personal* (as opposed to mere hypostatic) union. But rational natures are made in God's image and likeness and are capable of making deiformity explicit. Thus, hypostatic union with a donkey nature would not show forth God's power, goodness, and wisdom, in the way personal union with a rational nature would.[76] If excellence dictates choice of a rational as opposed to non-rational nature, why humans rather than angels? Bonaventure reaches back to the idea that human being is a microcosm, in which the rational soul represents God, not only in itself, but in the way it inhabits and reigns over its body as God does over the material world.[77]

(2) Nevertheless, if created rational natures have the capacity for deiformity, their natural powers are insufficient to produce it in and of themselves; Divine assistance is needed. Here Bonaventure faces a controversy over how God produces deiformity in a creature—whether by immediate Divine presence and/or by hypostatic union alone, or by being the

efficient cause that infuses some created habit into the creature itself. Guided by surface Biblical language, some held that the indwelling Holy Spirit was sufficient to organize and coordinate the exercise of the rational creature's powers, and that the immediately present Divine Word was sufficient for the creature's beatific knowledge.[78] Bonaventure insists that this language needs to be metaphysically "cashed," and argues that both deiformity and beatific knowledge require God to infuse a created habit in the soul. After all, God is omnipresent, but not all are deiform and not all see God.[79] Likewise, deiformity is *not posterior but prior* in the order of explanation to hypostatic union. Grace is required to dispose the will to conform to the regime of the Divine.[80]

4.2.1. Finite Fullness of Grace

For Bonaventure, deiformity is required for union with God on the part of any creature, and grace to conform the created will to the Divine is generally necessary for the blessed to see God and not just for the special case of personal union. But where Christ is concerned, Scripture and tradition specify fullness of grace. Bonaventure pauses to analyze what this means. Following Lombard's lead, Bonaventure reasons that because the soul of Christ is as much a creature as other human souls, and because the subjective capacity of creatures to receive inherent forms is finite, the habit of grace infused into Christ's soul must likewise be metaphysically finite.[81] Corollary to this, Bonaventure infers, the role of grace in disposing the soul for union with a Divine person is that of *congruent* rather than *condign* grace. If no created substance nature would be intrinsically and metaphysically commensurate with the Divine, *a fortiori* no created quality would make it metaphysically equal to the Divine essence.[82] All the same, since unity of person is the maximum unity possible between God and a creature, the soul of Christ should be as deiform as it is possible for a creature to be. Therefore, Bonaventure concludes, the soul of Christ had as intense a degree of grace as the subjective capacity of the human soul would allow, and so had not only the "deiformity of glory" that characterizes all of the blessed, but superabundant fullness beyond Stephen's "fullness of sufficiency" and Mary's "fullness of prerogative" and the "fullness of number or quantity" in the whole Church.[83]

In fact, Bonaventure maintains, the very same habit of grace that produces deiformity in Christ's soul and thereby fits it for unity of person with the Divine Word also suits Christ as God Incarnate for His role as head of the Church.[84] In corporeal things, the head of the body is of the same natural kind as the body, is the chief of its members, and the one that functions to influence the senses and motions of the others. Analogously, Christ is head of the Church, but both of His natures are involved. He is of the same natural kind according to His human nature, and He is the chief member because He is the source of all others according to His Divine nature. In spiritual things, what corresponds to sense is cognition, while motion has to do with affection and delight.[85] Fullness of grace in Christ's human nature puts Christ in a position to earn merit and to offer satisfaction to the severity of Divine justice, which in turn opens the flood gates for all of Christ's members to receive knowledge and delight that pertain to the state of glory. But Christ is the efficient cause of these benefits according to His Divine nature.[86]

4.2.2. Fullness of Knowledge

If like is known by like, maximal deiformity should mean fullness of knowledge. Unpacking this claim leads straight to the heart of Bonaventure's cognitive psychology. According to him, created intellectual cognition involves [i] a *ratio cognoscendi*, either in the object or its exemplar, [ii] a "formal influence" (a species or habit) in the cognizer who passively receives it, and [iii] an act of judgment by the cognizer in response to what it has received.[87] So far as seeing the Divine Word or seeing things in the Divine Word is concerned, Bonaventure identifies the Divine Word Itself as [i] the *ratio cognoscendi* both of the Divine Word and of those things of which the Divine Word is an exemplar.[88] The Divine Word is also [ii] the efficient cause of a habit in the soul by which the soul is made deiform and so conformed to the Divine Word Itself.[89] By means of this habit, the soul cognizes the Word Itself. By means of *the very same* habit, the soul has an habitual cognition of things of which the Word is exemplar.[90] If [iii] an act of judgment is involved in every cognition, when the Divine Word is seen, Bonaventure clarifies, the act of judgment does not evaluate the Divine Word, the fountain of all Truth, but rather the soul's cognition itself.[91]

If this account applies to all of the blessed and so to every soul who sees the Divine Word, Bonaventure notes—re [ii]—that the Divine Word represents what it represents to others *voluntarily*.[92] By infusing deiforming habits of differing degrees of perfection, the Divine Word controls how many other things the souls of the blessed see in the Divine Word. Bonaventure estimates that God wills that all of the blessed souls cognize not only the Divine Word but everything in the Divine Word that is essential to being in a state of glory, though not those others that are not essential to glory. And so, even the blessed will be able to think about things they have not considered before.[93] The soul of Christ receives special honors, however, in that the Divine Word does not will to make *everything* of which it is exemplar cognitively accessible to any but the soul of Christ.[94]

Bonaventure has emphasized that however hypostatically united to the Divine Word, the soul of Christ "remains within the bounds of a creature" as something finite and of finite power.[95] How, then, can it see [i] the Divine Word Who is intensively infinite, or [ii] the infinitely many creatures of which the Divine Word is the exemplar? Re [i], it seems that whatever a finite mind can "wrap itself around" would be circumscribed by the limits of the comprehending power.[96] But natural reason proves the Divine Word to be simple, so that cognition of it cannot be partial but rather must be "all or nothing."[97] Bonaventure rejects solutions that try to make the Divine essence finite because simple, or Christ's soul infinite by virtue of hypostatic union. Natural reason testifies against both proposals.[98] As to the simplicity-problem, Bonaventure struggles for analogies, but in the end he abandons hope of an adequate explanation of what reason in any event proves: viz., that God is cognized whole by any creature that cognizes Him, but is not wholly cognized.[99]

Re [ii], how could a finite human soul cognize an extensional infinity of creatures in the Divine Word? Bonaventure rejects the solution that the Divine Word cognizes finitely many because it is *exemplar* only with respect to the finitely many creatures actually made.[100] Likewise, Bonaventure denies that finite souls can *actually* cognize infinitely many because the single habit they receive from the Divine Word would be sufficient for this. For all of the blessed receive this habit, but only the soul of Christ is said to be omniscient.[101] Moreover, because cognition involves judgement, actually to know infinitely many would involve actual judgments with respect to infinitely many, which is likewise beyond a created soul's finite capacities.[102] Bonaventure identifies two solutions as defensible. The first distinguishes two senses of 'omniscience': the knowledge of vision that extends over all of the finitely many that God is disposed to make; and knowledge of intelligence that ranges over the infinitely many each of which God can make. This solution then construes the omniscience of Christ's finite human soul in terms of the knowledge of vision rather than knowledge of intelligence. Bonaventure harbors the lingering doubt that this position is overly restrictive. Even if the human soul of Christ could not actually think of infinitely many simultaneously, why couldn't it think of some of the things God has not actually made but could create?[103]

The position Bonaventure prefers relies instead on twin distinctions between actual and habitual cognition on the one hand, and between what a habit is essentially in itself and its relations (*respectus*) to the objects of cognition on the other. Bonaventure contends that there is no problem with a habit, finite quality though it be, being related to infinitely many objects simultaneously. On this suggestion, because the Divine will wills the soul of Christ to have cognitive access to the infinitely many possibles of which It is the exemplar, the Divine Word supplies the soul of Christ with just such a habit, so that the soul of Christ habitually cognizes infinitely many. No new habit will be required for it actually to consider something it has not actually considered before, for it will be able to "read whatever It wants to" there.[104] It can consider each, but it never will consider all.[105]

4.2.3. Straddling the Stages!

Like Lombard, Bonaventure appropriates Boethius' claim that Christ recapitulates by telescoping human history—i.e., by taking something from each of its stages. But Bonaventure recognizes that this idea spawns complications, not least among which is a superfluity of knowledge in the soul of Christ. We have just seen how the "deiformity of glory" produced by the Divine Word in the soul of Christ is sufficient both for habitual omniscience and for actual cognition of the Divine Word and whatever else is essential to glory. So far as the range of knowables is concerned, this would have been enough. But cognitive perfection in the soul of Christ has somehow to represent [i] all of the states of human being: in particular, the cognition of the whole nature, and the cognition of penal experience;[106] [ii] all modes of knowing: knowing things as they are in the Word, as they exist in the created intellect, and as they are in themselves; and [iii] all of the powers: not only superior reason, but also inferior reason and the senses.[107] This means that besides cognizing things in the Word, the soul of Christ cognizes things via species infused into It at its creation, in the way Adam did before the fall and in the way the angels always do.[108] Likewise, the soul of Christ has experiential cognition, which involves the use of its sensory powers and the exercise of reason to consider and make judgments about such sensory deliverances.[109] The soul of Christ does not, however, join *post-lapsum* humans in abstracting species from material conditions, because it already has a full supply.[110]

So far as learning or growth in knowledge is concerned, the fullness of its knowledge in the Divine Word makes it impossible for the soul of Christ to acquire any fresh speculative knowledge, but it does not prevent it from knowing speculative items in a new way.[111] Likewise, the soul of Christ can actually consider for the first time what it knew only habitually and can apply the dictates of reason to new sensory experiences.[112]

4.2.4. Fullness of Power?

Does deiformity bring with it fullness of power? Bonaventure's reasons for saying "no" point to the metaphysically necessary lack of aseity and simplicity in creatures. Creatures fall short of maximal stability, because they lack the power to sustain their own existence. Creatures fall short of maximal simplicity and so lack the power to act through themselves as a whole. Creatures fall short of maximal immensity, so that their substances cannot be identical with their powers.

Because it is metaphysically possible (indeed metaphysically necessary) for something to possess such powers, and because they imply no imperfection, creatures cannot possess fullness of power or be omnipotent.[113]

4.3. The Assumed Nature, How Defective?

In Christ, deiformity is "fitting for Him," indeed presupposed for the congruence of hypostatic union; but defects are "useful to us." True to his Franciscan devotion, Bonaventure has identified Christ's principal soteriological job as that of making satisfaction for sin through His suffering and death on the cross. And this involves a certain degree of identification with Adam's race.[114] Bonaventure thinks it is "doubtless" true that the Son of God could have taken flesh from elsewhere, but argues that it is more fitting for Christ to take it from Adam's race for a medley of Anselmian reasons.[115]

4.3.1. Assuming Adam?

More startling is Bonaventure's consideration of the suggestion that the Divine Word should have assumed the first man, Adam himself! *Justice* seems to favor it, because one man ought not to take another's punishment.[116] *Wisdom* favors the efficiency of it, since satisfaction made by Adam would be passed on to the whole human race that descends from his loins.[117] *The principles of medicine* support it, because it would strike the disease of corruption in its Adamic root.[118]

Patristic and medieval precedents make it predictable that Bonaventure would reject this challenging proposal on *soteriological* grounds. For the Son of God to assume Adam would be, by *communicatio idiomatum,* for God to become a sinner and thereby to be disqualified for His role as judge of sinners. It would also mean that Adam gained by his fall, with his guilt being rewarded by the highest honor of hypostatic union. In any event, that man would be guilty and owe punishment, and therefore would be unqualified to make satisfaction.[119] As for the comparison of the Incarnation with the Holy Spirit's descending upon and indwelling guilty souls, Bonaventure sees twin disanalogies. The Holy Spirit is an *efficient* while Christ is a *meritorious* cause in the purification of sinners. Likewise, because the Holy Spirit is not hypostatically united to the guilty souls it indwells, there is no *communicatio idiomatum* between them, as there is in the Incarnation.[120] Thus, in Bonaventure's estimation, assuming Adam would be too much and the wrong kind of identification with Adam's race—neither fitting for God nor expedient for us!

What Bonaventure does not notice are the *metaphysical* difficulties involved in this idea as well as in the Seraphic Doctor's critique. For either 'Adam' stands for a person/supposit, or for the individual human nature. It is metaphysically impossible for one person/supposit to assume another person/supposit. Therefore, it is metaphysically impossible for the Son of God to become the person who sinned and owed the punishment, or for Adam to profit personally by becoming the Son of God. What can be assumed is the individual human nature. If it were cleansed upon arrival by the efficient causal activity of the Holy Spirit or the Divine Word or the Trinity Itself, then there would be no sinful act in the nature to be attributed to the Divine supposit, and God would not be a sinner by *communicatio idiomatum*. True, cleansing could not make it the case that a sinful act had never inhered in the assumed soul. But if sin and guilt belong to the supposit, properly speaking, this would not imply that the Son of God is a sinner. For the nature would have belonged to someone else at the time of the sin, and that supposit would no longer exist. The Son of God would turn out to be a sinner only if there were a sinful act in the human soul of the assumed nature while it belonged to Him!

4.3.2. *Posse Peccare?*

If the Son of God could not assume an actual sinner, doesn't He have at least to take to Himself the possibility of sinning? Philosophically—*pace* Anselm

—the ability to sin seems not to be a defect but rather to be partially constitutive of the freedom that is a necessary condition of praise or blame, merit or demerit.[121] Theologically, *posse peccare* is characteristic of the state of the *viator* into which Adam's race fell.[122] Bonaventure agrees that the human soul of Christ has free choice, which essentially includes a power for opposites and hence a power for turning and defecting. But Christ cannot actually defect, because—as Lombard claimed—Christ occupies all of the states of human being at once. Deiformity of glory brings fullness of grace that so conforms free choice in its Godward orientation that it cannot be weakened by guilt (*non posse peccare*)![123] Once again, appealing to *communicatio idiomatum*, Bonaventure warns that power to sin in Christ's human soul would mean that it is possible for God to sin.[124]

4.3.3. Vulnerability and Weakness

If neither actual nor possible guilt is to any purpose, surely other defects are prerequisite for Christ's saving work. Would not Christ have to take from our fallen state the defect of passibility, indeed of actual participation in our misery, humiliation, and death? Are these not the currency with which he earns merit and makes satisfaction for sin? Aren't they the sacrifice which he offers as our compassionate high priest?[125] Others disagree, insisting, once again, that justice forbids punishment of the innocent; that curing our weakness and conquering the adversary requires, not vulnerability, but impassibility and strength.[126]

Bonaventure removes the contrary considerations with a series of distinctions. First, there are *two types of punishment*. *Vindictive punishment* is inflicted on the guilty willy nilly and is appropriately imposed only on the guilty. *Placating punishment*, however, is voluntarily assumed and does not presuppose guilt in the person who takes the penalties but rather in the one on whose behalf s/he volunteers. Bonaventure declares that the severity of Divine justice is better pleased by the voluntary suffering of the innocent on behalf of the guilty than by any punishment of the unjust and the guilty.[127] Second, Bonaventure contrasts *natural strength* and *moral strength*. Natural weakness and vulnerability "can be matter for the exercise of virtue. For the virtue of courage is exercised most strongly in the midst of terrible things, of which those that lead to death are the worst."[128] Likewise, such hardships are occasions for *humility and patience,* through which the devil and sin are conquered.[129]

However incongruous weakness and vulnerability may seem in themselves, Bonaventure reaffirms three soteriological roles for which they are essential. First and most importantly, they are necessary for Christ to pay the price of our redemption through His suffering and death. Second, weakness and vulnerability are required for Christ to give us an example of the virtues—chiefly, humility, patience, and piety—by means of which we reach heaven. Third, weakness and vulnerability are presupposed if Christ's life is to illustrate how a grace-assisted human being can persevere to the end. Christ's example strengthens us in our weakness, insofar as it gives reason occasion to believe the truth about human nature and its grace-assisted capacities. Christ gives irascible nature reason to hope in the midst of hardship. Christ's benevolence towards us in His passion and death incite concupiscible nature to love what is most worth loving.[130] Yet, Christ does not have to assume every defect known to man in order to get these jobs done. Bonaventure sorts which are which through a further distinction between *natural* defects that are essential to human being generally (e.g., hunger and thirst) and *personal* defects (e.g., blindness, lameness, being hunched-backed) that befall some humans and not others. Relative to the tasks Bonaventure singles out, it is the natural defects that prove useful. Obvious material for virtue that many other defects are, Bonaventure dismisses them as on balance counterproductive.[131]

Nor does Christ come by these natural human defects the same way as we do. Bonaventure takes over Lombard's claim that we inherit them by natural propagation from fallen human parents,[132] whereas Christ assumes them voluntarily. But Bonaventure underlines the further point that the penalty of passibility is retained, not only by an act of the Divine will, but also by the consent of Christ's human will at the first instant of its creation.[133] Once Christ's double consent is given, however, the nature of the passible body, composed as it is of contraries, brings with it the necessity of suffering.[134]

4.3.4. Ignorance, Merely Apparent?

Bonaventure argues that the defect of ignorance is unfitting for Christ, not only because it is incompatible with the deiformity presupposed for hypostatic union, but also because it could lead to error and falling away from justice. Likewise, ignorance in Christ's soul would be an obstacle to His redeeming us from ignorance and so not be useful to us.[135]

4.4. Appetites at Odds?

One liability under which fallen humans labor is divided appetites. For Bonaventure, human nature is complex, joining two substances—mind and body—in one individual. The soul has sensory as well as rational appetites, which pull in different directions. With Christ, won't it be all the more so? He has a Divine as well as a human nature: in addition to all of the human appetites, the Divine will as well.[136] Doesn't the Bible itself record how Christ wept over Jerusalem, whose destruction the Divine will ordained; how he begged in the Garden, "Not my will but thine"? Weren't Christ's human sensibilities—terror and flight—opposed to His own rational consent to the passion?[137]

For his part, Bonaventure reaffirms the distinction of human and Divine wills in Christ against the twentieth-century style objection that two wills make for two willers, and so two personalities. Bonaventure counters that 'person' does not mark an organ of thought and volition, but the supposit of a rational nature. Following medieval construals of Chalcedon, he insists that the doctrine of the Incarnation surprises us with the information that two rational natures can simultaneously be supposited by one supposit. Hence, one person, (at least) two wills![138]

Echoing Lombard with slightly different terminology, Bonaventure complicates the plurality of appetitive directions in Christ by distinguishing *reason as reason,* whose object is the outcome of deliberation, and *reason as nature,* which is a natural inclination to the body the soul perfects.[139] Bonaventure agrees that—most notably with regard to His passion—the different wills in Christ have *different objects.* But he elegantly dissolves the *prima facie* problem this causes by recognizing two ways for wills to be in conformity with each other: either by having the same objects, or by being subordinated to one another so that the lower will wills what the higher wills it to will and so that the higher prevails in directing the individual's action. The deiformity of Christ insures that His wills are appropriately subordinated to one another—the sensory and the rational-as-nature to deliberative reason; deliberative reason to the Divine will. Thus, Christ's sensory appetites and His reason-as-nature can nill His suffering and death, while His rational deliberation will rejoice over it. Yet, each wills what God wills it to will, because God wills them to will different objects according to their different functional roles in human being.[140] Christ wills are harmonized by being properly "hierarchized," but not by having the same objects.

4.5. The Passions of the Soul

This understanding shapes Bonaventure's treatment of sensory appetites and passions in Christ in predictable and traditional ways. In each, he distinguishes *a feeling component* that arises in the individual by natural necessity, from the impact the occurrence of this feeling has upon reason's rule in the soul. Because Christ's appetites are always properly hierarchized, sensory appetites and passions will never be able to cloud His mind or overthrow reason's rule.[141]

So far as the *Sentence*-commentary format allows it, Bonaventure rushes through his discussions of anger and *tristitia*[142] to dwell on *dolor*, that passion of the soul he deems most central to Christ's saving work on the cross. By contrast with *tristitia, dolor* seems to be more associated with the soul's conjunction with a passible body, and with the mutual interaction of soul and body on the one hand and of the soul's powers on the other. Bonaventure begins with the *dolor* that is the sorrow of a soul that is really suffering with the passible body to which it is conjoined. Bonaventure emphasizes that though the soul finds an occasion for this *dolor* in bodily harms, the soul itself really suffers when the occasion is taken.[143] This *dolor*, Bonaventure says, occurs primarily in the soul's sensory powers.[144]

Against "the heretics and Saracens," Bonaventure contends that Christ really had passible, pierceable flesh, and a real power of sensing according to which His soul suffered from His body's wounds. The two—a real wound and a real sensing of the wound—make for real *dolor*. This was for Christ the material of the patience which He displayed in His passion. To deny this, Bonaventure declares, "would not only evacuate the faith of Christ and the Gospel of Christ, but also our redemption."[145] It would be to "say that Christ is not Christ" because it would imply that "Christ did not make satisfaction." Again, Bonaventure threatens, "the one who says that he simulated suffering says that He is a liar and so was not truly the Son of God or messenger of God, and so not the mediator but a deceiver." Thus, while it might *prima facie* seem more honoring to Christ to make Him invulnerable to *dolor*, it is in fact blasphemy and impiety!

Returning to a more analytical mode, Bonaventure draws the further consequence that because Christ's bodily complexion was of the noblest sort and His senses as lively as possible, this sensory *dolor* was of the most acute order possible.[146] Bonaventure also recognizes how sensory *dolor* spills over to afflict reason-as-nature, which—as a natural appetite to perfect the body—delights in the well-being of the body and sorrows in its injury. Thus, reason-as-nature suffers as sensuality suffers when the body is damaged.[147]

Further, Bonaventure acknowledges another sort of *dolor* that afflicts the soul in itself. Deliberative reason sorrows over conditions it nills, so that Christ suffers over our dishonor to and consequent separation from God.[148] In fact, Bonaventure says that this *dolor* was for Him the most intense, because its causes were the more serious: sin and sinners' separation from God are much more grievous than the separation of soul from body.[149] But deliberative reason does not sorrow alone; its compassion overflows into sensuality, so that when reason suffers, the senses cry out![150]

4.6. Appetites and States

Bonaventure's analysis of *dolor* manages to appreciate the unity of human being, his metaphysical mind-body dualism notwithstanding. For Bonaventure, the human soul is no aloof pilot directing a ship through rocky shoals. No, the soul hurts when the body hurts; when reason is distressed, the senses cry out. In this discussion, Bonaventure also displays his steadfast commitment to the reality of Christ's human nature, not only of mind but also of passible and pierceable body, not only of its rational but also of its sensory powers. Yet, while Bonaventure's appeal to hierarchy elegantly handles the *prima facie* problem of multiple appetites with different objects, the drive to locate *dolor* not only in the senses but also in reason causes problems for the human psychology of Christ. For according to Bonaventure, Christ's rational appetite experiences *dolor* twice over. Most intense is that of deliberative reason over sin and its consequences. But Christ's reason-as-nature is acutely afflicted at the damage to His body and the suffering of His senses, and this suffering is also of very high degree due to the keenness of Christ's sensory powers. That Christ's real human faculties are fully engaged in suffering His passion and death is necessary—Bonaventure thinks—for our salvation. Nevertheless, Bonaventure makes deformity of glory prerequisite for hypostatic union. And this means that Christ enjoys a beatific vision of the

Divine Word in His human soul from the first instant of His creation. The problem is that joy and
sorrow, happiness and misery seem to be contraries.
How can Christ experience both, mutually undi-
minished, in the same rational faculty at once?[151]

Bonaventure struggles with this difficulty, but
eventually wins through to what he takes to be a
promising approach based on three "defensible" assumptions. (1) First, despite appearances, the joy
and sorrow in question are not really contraries,
because they are not about the same object and do
not pertain to their subject (the soul) in altogether
the same way. The joy is in seeing *God* and arises
because of its hypostatic union with the Divine
Word. The sorrow is about us, about our sin and
separation from God, and about His own bodily
torments and death, and arises because of the natural conjunction of the soul with the body.[152] While
helpful, this suggestion by itself might not be fully
satisfying from the point of view of experience. Don't
we often find that intense sorrow (or joy) about one
thing interferes with intense joy (or sorrow) about
another? (2) The second thesis goes some way towards meeting this concern, with its observation that
this *dolor*, so far from necessarily interfering with,
may itself be the material for rejoicing, whether in
the penitent who is glad to suffer for his own sins,
or in Christ Who rejoiced over His passion and death
for the salvation of the world.[153] (3) The third claim
seems more helpful still: viz., that deformity ex-
pands the soul's natural capacity so that it can be
wholly turned towards and differently affected by
multiple objects at once.[154] Such psychic enlarge-

ment is really presupposed by the Lombardian dictum that Christ recapitulates by simultaneously telescoping into Himself all of the states of human being. Having insisted in the abstract that two wills do not mean two persons, Bonaventure now admits that for Christ to be in two of the states of human being at once—on the one hand, to experience the bitter suffering of our sin and alienation, the acute torment of His passion and death; and on the other, to enjoy a beatific vision of God—is as if (*quasi*) for Him to be two persons! This is how great the psychic expansion will have to be if the cognitions and affections of a *viator* are not to obstruct the vision and enjoyment of glory.[155] But given Bonaventure's earlier sensitivity to the natural receptive capacities of the created human soul, it is surprising that he does not pause to ponder whether the augmentation here envisioned is really metaphysically possible.

V. Aquinas' Analysis

In his *Summa theologiæ*, Aquinas joins Anselm in squarely confronting objections from Divine dignity to the propriety of the Incarnation. Unlike Anselm, Aquinas opposes infidel inferences from the metaphysical "size-gap" with Pseudo-Dionysius' conception of God as self-diffusing Goodness. What is fitting or proper for an agent to do is a function of its nature. If God's nature is self-diffusing Goodness, it is fitting for God to share Divine Goodness with others. God does this in creation insofar as He pours the goodness of existence (*esse*) into created natures, each of which is an imperfect likeness of Divine Goodness.[156] But the Divine nature would be maximally shared if some Divine person joined itself to a created nature in unity of person. Therefore, it was fitting for God to be incarnate.[157] In *Summa contra Gentiles*, Book IV, c.55, Aquinas goes on to explain how it is especially fitting that the Godhead join itself to human nature because by joining Godself to a nature at the metaphysical borderline between physical and spiritual, God symbolically unites Godself to the whole of creation. Even if angelic natures are better imitations of Divine Goodness, uniting with human nature enables God to join heaven to earth and earth to heaven![158]

Nevertheless, by the time of the *Summa theologiæ*, Aquinas is unwilling to ride the momentum of this picture to the further conclusion that God *would* have become Incarnate even if humans had not sinned. Certainly, he admits, Divine power *could* have done so.[159] But "in Sacred Scriptures the reason for the Incarnation is everywhere assigned to the sin of the first human."[160] Where for Bonaventure the authorities' silence as to other motivations was but one consideration among others, Aquinas solidifies his refusal to go further into a methodological posture. Aquinas shares with Anselm the sense that Divine Goodness is unfathomable *a priori*. The argument for the propriety of the Incarnation proceeds, not *a priori*, but *a posteriori* from the data of creation and Incarnation, disclosed by natural reason and revelation, respectively. But we cannot know about matters that proceed from the Divine will alone beyond anything required for creatures, unless they are handed down to us in the Sacred Scriptures. And—like Bonaventure—Aquinas denies that hypostatic union with a Divine person is required for the *natural* perfection of creatures individually or collectively. Rather, created capacity for such hypostatic union *exceeds* their *natural* capacities and is merely a matter of the *obediential* potency of creatures to serve functions of the Divine will.[161] Given the silence of the Bible on what would have happened had Adam never fallen, Aquinas concludes,

> it is more appropriate to say that the work of Incarnation is ordered by God for the remedy of sin in such a way that were there no sin, there would have been no Incarnation.[162]

> ...For if humans had not sinned, they would have been flooded with the light of Divine Wisdom and perfected by the uprightness of justice from God in order to know everything necessary. But because humans, having deserted God, fell into corporeal things, it was fitting that God, having assumed flesh, also exhibit the remedy through corporeal things.[163]

Unsurprisingly, then, Aquinas calculates the features of the assumed nature from what is "mete and right" for leading Adam's fallen race back to the perfection intended by God.

5.1. Fullness of Grace

For Aquinas as for Lombard, Christ as prototype and head pioneers human excellence—both natural and supernatural—by exemplifying it, to a large extent even during His earthly career.[164] If union with God is the human end, Christ's human nature enjoys it from its beginning by virtue of the Incarnation.[165] Appealing to causal analogies, Aquinas explains that grace is caused in humans by the presence of Divinity, just as light is produced in the air by the presence of the sun.[166] Again, the intensity and excellence of an effect is a function of the patient's proximity to the causal agent.[167] Because hypostatic union places Christ's human nature as close as any creature can come to the Divine essence, fullness of habitual grace beams into His soul like splendor from the sun.[168] Again, just as God is fontal source of natural being (*esse*) and goodness in creatures, so Aquinas envisions a cascading flow of grace: from Godhead into the human soul hypostatically united to it; from the soul of Christ into all the members of the Body of which He is the head.[169] Indeed, Aquinas declares, these latter include the whole human race in all times and all places, whose members themselves form a descending hierarchy in proportion to their union with Christ—from [i] the closest (the blessed angels and saints) who are united to Him through glory; to [ii] those who are actually united to Him through *charity*; down to [iii] those who are *actually* united through *faith*; and further to [iv] those who are *as yet only potentially* united because Divine predestination certifies their *future actual* union; and finally to [v] humans created but not predestined by God, whose potential for union with Christ will never be actualized.[170] There is a difference, however. For if Aquinas sees the flow of grace into the soul of Christ as a *natural* consequence of its hypostatic union with the Divine Word, its flooding into other creatures is not a *natural* process but rather one that depends on Divine choice to confer grace and to distribute it first through Christ and secondarily through the institutional structures of the Church.[171]

5.2. Surplus Knowledge

Christ as head and forerunner must lead the human race to that fullness of knowledge of which humans are capable *qua* images of God. Once again drawing on causal models, Aquinas pictures Christ "catching" perfection from God and passing it down to others. Accordingly, he reminds us that "what is in potency is reduced to act only through what is in act" and concludes that the soul of Christ must have such knowledge *ab initio*.

Beginning with the supernatural, Aquinas reasons that Christ's human knowledge will exceed that of any other created knowers, because "the soul of Christ is more closely joined to the Word of God than any other creatures" and "therefore receives a fuller influence of that light in which God is seen from the Word Itself."[172] Again, looking down to what it causes rather than up to what produces it, Aquinas infers that because (in this case?) the cause is more powerful than the effect, Christ must have beatific knowledge of God in the most excellent degree possible for creatures.[173] Like Bonaventure,

Aquinas acknowledges that the "size-gap" between
God and creatures means that the soul of Christ
cannot *comprehend* the Divine essence: while the
former sees *the whole* of the latter,[174] the soul's capacity to see does not exhaust Divinity's capacity to
be seen.[175]

Like Lombard and Bonaventure, Aquinas wants
to acknowledge that no created intelligence can
match the Creator's cognitive capacities, and yet to
maintain that, in seeing God, the soul of Christ sees
not only God but creatures in the Divine Word.
On the one hand, Aquinas picks up Lombard's point
that knowledge is measured not only by how many
objects it grasps but also by the *clarity* with which it
apprehends them.[176] On the other, Aquinas embraces
the first of Bonaventure's options, distinguishing
between God's *knowledge of vision* (Divine knowledge insofar as it ranges over everything that ever
did, does, or ever will actually exist) and God's *knowledge of simple intelligence* (Divine knowledge insofar
as it ranges not only over things that actually exist
at some time, but also everything that *can* exist,
whether by created or Divine power).[177] Any and all
of the blessed will know what God knows by knowledge of vision,[178] and the human soul of Christ will
know mere possibles that lie within created powers.[179] But Aquinas insists that full knowledge of
simple intelligence is impossible for any creature
because it is allegedly tantamount to *comprehending*
Divine power and so comprehending the Divine essence.[180]

Like Augustine and Bonaventure, Aquinas denies
that seeing God and knowing creatures in the Di-

vine Word renders the *natural* functioning of Christ's human intellect otiose.[181] But Aquinas' development of this point is shaped by his own contrasting cognitive psychology. For Aquinas takes the knowledge of the blessed to be unmediated by intelligible species and so to involve immediate cognitive union of the knower with God; and he takes an Aristotelian turn in analyzing natural human understanding in terms of the agent intellect's capacity to abstract from phantasms and to impress intelligible species on the possible intellect that has the capacity to receive them. Aquinas contends that these two types of knowledge are as different in kind as sensory cognition is from intellectual cognition, so that having both of the former is no more impossible than having both of the latter.[182] Moreover, Christ could not lead human nature to its Divinely intended dignity if His own highest natural powers were simply displaced.

So far as the created intellect's passive capacity to receive intelligible species is concerned, Aquinas joins Bonaventure in insisting that God treats Christ's human soul like angelic intellects, by infusing into it a full supply of intelligible species at the first moment of its creation.[183] In terms of Aquinas' Aristotelian cognitive psychology, this means that Christ's possible intellect is infused with as many intelligible species as it could have possibly received from the agent intellect.[184] To the worry that this is *unnatural* for bottom-of-the-line human intellects whose proper object is the quiddities of material things[185] and which naturally understand only by turning to phantasms,[186] Aquinas seems even to modify the cognitive psychology that grounded his arguments that the soul is the form of the body and—though subsistent—will not *post mortem* remain forever separated from it. What sounded in *Prima Pars* like natural necessity now is treated as a present and temporary condition of the soul's being bound to the body.[187] *Post mortem* the soul will in no way be subordinate to or dependent upon the body but will wholly dominate it.[188] Even *ante mortem*, Christ's human soul participates in this cognitive independence of phantasms by virtue of His supernaturally infused intelligible species.[189]

Where Bonaventure concedes that there will be no naturally produced intelligible species in the soul of Christ, Aquinas insists that there must be. How exemplary could Christ's human nature be, if His *agent* intellect, arguably the finest of His human cognitive powers, never engaged in its function? In response, Aquinas introduces a further redundancy of knowledge. Besides seeing creatures in the Divine Word and knowing them by means of supernaturally infused species, Christ's human soul is said to be able to *acquire* knowledge by experience, in which His agent intellect abstracts intelligible species from phantasms.[190] The possession of species confers *habitual* rather than *exercised* knowledge; to move from the former to the latter requires a command of the will.[191] *Pace* Bonaventure, Aquinas implies that infused and acquired habits of knowledge can co-exist with respect to the same objects, because infused and acquired habits are themselves different in kind.[192]

If Christ's role as prototype and head drives Aquinas to assert the supremacy of His human knowledge in relation to other members of Adam's race, how does it compare with the angels' knowledge? "A little lower"[193] so far as its *natural* mode of human cognition is concerned; but "crowned with glory and honor" because the "spiritual light infused on the soul of Christ was more excellent than that which pertains to angelic intellects."[194]

Is *growth* in any of Christ's knowledge possible (*à la* Luke 2:52)? Predictably, Aquinas replies that neither Christ's beatific knowledge of God and of creatures in God, nor any habit of infused knowledge admits of augmentation, because these are maximal to begin with; but habits of acquired knowledge can be intensified via further acts of abstraction from phantasms.[195] Nevertheless, it does not befit Christ's dignity either to learn from other humans[196] or to acquire knowledge from angels.[197]

5.3. Omnipotence, a Divine Prerogative

Aquinas' claims about Christ's human knowledge posit in the human soul a remarkable *passive* capacity to receive information in the form of supernaturally caused acts of seeing God and all things in God, as well as a full set of supernaturally caused intelligible species. Like Lombard, he finds differences between Divine and created natural capacities more telling where *active* power is concerned. According to Aquinas, it is because the Divine essence *is* unbounded being (*esse*) that its active power extends to whatever can have the aspect of being (i.e., that it is omnipotent). Nothing that is not uncircumscribed being (*esse*) could be omnipotent—and this includes Christ's human nature, whose powers are circumscribed by its own limited being (*esse*).[198] Most importantly, the human nature of Christ—like every other finite being—lacks the power to create *ex nihilo*.[199]

Even if the power of Christ's human nature is no match for the Divine, would it not exceed that of other creatures,[200] extending to any and all changes (*immutationes*) in the creaturely world?[201] Is this not shown by His performance of signs and wonders during His earthly career?[202] Here Aquinas distinguishes between the human soul considered in itself and qua instrument of Divine power. As to the first way, Aquinas need only repeat: because *active* power follows nature, Christ's human soul has the same natural capacity as any other human soul—e.g., power to govern the body, dispose its human acts, illuminate phantasms, etc.[203] As to the second way, Christ's human nature has power to do whatever the Divine Word can use it as an instrument to do. Here again, causal principles and analogies shape Aquinas' intuitions. Elsewhere he distinguishes external instruments (e.g., the pool stick I use to sink the eight ball) from internal instruments (e.g., bodily members such as hand and arm are the soul's instruments), and characterizes the human nature of Christ as an internal instrument of the Divine Word which assumes it. Likewise, he insists that instruments enjoy a temporary and transient participation in the power (*virtus*) of the principal agent while they are being used. Thus, the human soul of Christ, considered as an instrument of the Divine Word, participates in Divine power, which is the principal agent in the miracles worked through it—which would include some but not all of the miracles God does (e.g., the raising of Lazarus, but not stopping the sun for the battle of Jericho).[204]

Still, if Christ is to lead Adam's race back to perfection, shouldn't His soul be omnipotent with respect to His own body? After all, Adam's body was fully subject to his soul in the state of original justice before the fall?[205] Once again, Aquinas' conservative estimates are governed by the principle that the human soul has a determinate proportion to its own body.[206] Even in Eden, Adam did not have active power to change his own body with respect to any and every form, but only power to *conserve* the form he had from harm.[207] Likewise, considered in itself, Christ's human soul has no more power to alter the natural dispositions of His own body than it does to change the natural course of other bodies. *Qua* instrument of the Divine Word, however, every disposition of His body is totally subordinate to His power.[208]

5.4. Satisfying Defects!

Other things being equal, Christ's role as prototype and head demands as much perfection as human nature is supernaturally capable of. But this theoretical presumption has to be balanced against the requirements of other aspects of Christ's saving work. Aquinas recognizes three soteriological jobs that presuppose a mixture of perfection and defects in Christ's human nature: making satisfaction, advertising the reality of the Incarnation, and furnishing an example of patience.[209] With Anselm, Lombard, and Bonaventure, Aquinas observes the methodological rule of assigning to Christ only those human defects that are necessary for His saving work.[210]

Like Anselm and Bonaventure, Aquinas identifies Christ's root task with making satisfaction for sin. Where Anselm argued that the Incarnation is *hypothetically necessary*—given human sin—for the fulfillment of Divine purpose, so that Christ's passion and death are *a necessary means* thereto; Aquinas distinguishes two ways in which something may be *necessary for an end*—either [i] as a *sine qua non* condition, or [ii] as a *better or more appropriate* means to an end,[211] and he maintains that the Incarnation, passion, and death of Christ are necessary only in the second sense.[212] Aquinas denies—*pace* Anselm—that Divine justice absolutely requires satisfaction. Human judges cannot justly dismiss guilt or punishment for a crime committed against another human or the whole republic or a higher prince. But King David did injury to no one when he dismissed an offense against himself. *A fortiori*, God, Who has no superior and is the supreme and common good of the whole universe, can forgive sins against Himself without injustice.[213] Nevertheless, Aquinas thinks God has decided on the more severe policy to which He is also (like relevantly positioned humans) entitled. Yet, in doing so, God has been able to integrate many other benefits along the way.

More than once, Aquinas declares that making satisfaction requires Christ to have perfecting habits—indeed, perfect knowledge and virtue—in His human soul, and defects in His human body.[214] In fact, the details are messier, but acquire definition along Lombardian lines.

(1) Bodily Defects

For Aquinas, Christ's making satisfaction involves undergoing the punishments for sin that others deserved, and corporeal defects are among the penalties consequent upon Adam's fall.[215] Like Bonaventure, Aquinas distinguishes some that are common to all (viz., susceptibility to hunger, thirst, and death)[216] from others that result from particular occasions (e.g., leprosy, fatal falls from high places)[217] or from defects in functioning of the generative powers.[218] The last category does not apply because the omnipotent Holy Spirit was the active cause in forming Christ's human nature. Along with Bonaventure, Aquinas claims that taking the common defects will be enough not only for making satisfaction, but also for demonstrating the reality of His human nature[219] and furnishing an example of patience in bodily suffering.[220]

Like Lombard, Aquinas recognizes a difficulty in how even this threesome of corporeal defects would be possible in a human nature with such perfections of soul. A special miracle will have to obstruct—on grounds of soteriological expediency—the natural tendency for the glory of the soul to redound to the body.[221] Again, Christ assumes the mortal, passible body voluntarily—not out of necessity due to *personal* guilt[222]—but once assumed it is the nature of that body to be vulnerable to puncturing by nails, cutting by whips, etc.[223]

(2) Immunity from Sin

Like Bonaventure, Aquinas is emphatic that sin in Christ's human soul would disqualify Him for His saving work. Sin is an obstacle to making satisfaction and a counter-example to virtue. As a defect in human nature it is not even an apt way to demonstrate the reality of the Incarnation.[224]

Nevertheless, because Scripture could seem to weigh in on the other side, he pauses to domesticate proof-texts that pull the other way. [i] Does not Christ's own quotation (Mt 27:46) of Psalm 22:1—"My God, my God, why have you forsaken me?"—evidence distress and a sense of abandonment, which would qualify as sin?[225] Aquinas' answer repeats Damascene's strategy: Christ made the remark not about Himself as Head, but about His Body, the Church.[226] [ii] Does not Hebrews 2:18—"because Christ suffered and was tempted, He was able to help us who are tempted"—imply that Christ's power to help us depends on His identification with our condition? Maximal aid against sin would require Him to identify with us in sin. Aquinas replies that Christ helps our sinful condition through His passion and trials by which He makes satisfaction for us. Personal sin on His part would nullify their effectiveness.[227] [iii] What about II Corinthians 5:21—"God made Him to be sin Who knew no sin,"[228] or Isaiah 53:6—"The Lord put on Him the iniquities of us all"?[229] Aquinas defends his reading—that God handed Christ over to be the sacrifice for sin.[230] In his *Galatians-Commentary*, Aquinas takes a similar approach with Galatians 3:13—"Christ redeemed us from the curse of the law, having become curse for us—for it is written, 'cursed be every one who hangs on a tree' [Dt 21:23]." Distinguishing between the curse of guilt and the curse of punishment, Aquinas explains that Christ redeemed us from the evil of guilt by becoming the curse of guilt simply in the sense that *the Jews regarded Him as the worst type of criminal.*[231] On the other hand, Christ is said to have become the curse of punishment in the sense that He endured the curse of punishment and death that came upon us through sin, and thereby freed us from it. Expounding Paul's own proof-text (Dt 21:23), Aquinas first raises a philological consideration:

> according to a Gloss, that in Deuteronomy, from which this passage is taken, our version as well as the Hebrew version has: "Cursed by God is everyone that hangs on a tree." *However, the phrase "by God" is not found in the ancient Hebrew volumes. Hence it is believed to have been added by the Jews after the passion of Christ in order to defame Him.*[232]

Alternatively, one could construe the passage in terms of the curse of guilt attributed to Him by those who hung Him there and the curse of punishment which He suffered.[233] Confronting the passage in *Summa theologiæ* III, he simply declares that sin and death are cursed on the cross, not Christ![234]

(3) Incarnational Action Theory—Appetites Vulnerable or Conforming?

If Chalcedon stipulated two unconfused natures in Christ: Divine and human—a human soul as well as a human body—the Sixth Synod of Constantinople made it explicit that there must be a human will as much as a Divine. Aquinas accepts this without hesitation.[235] Drawing on his own analysis of human nature, Aquinas maintains that the soul of Christ wills its end by natural necessity, but has free choice with respect to its means.[236] Moreover, he recognizes a sensory appetite alongside the rational appetite of Christ's human soul.[237] Like Bonaventure, Aquinas takes perfect virtue and sinlessness to imply the appropriate coordination—more precisely, *subordination*—of these appetites to one another: the sensory to the rational, the rational to the Divine. Defining *'fomes peccati'* as sensory appetitive inclinations to what is contrary to right reason, Aquinas denies Christ's soul any participation in these.[238] Thus, Christ furnishes an example of spiritual courage, not by experiencing carnal lust, but by so dominating His flesh that it does not lust against the spirit, and by perseverance in His outer struggle with the world and the devil.[239] Again, perfect prudence rules out agonizing equivocation between reasons *pro* and *con*.[240]

Still, for Aquinas as for Bonaventure, *perfect* subordination does not mean that the appetites never conflict. It is the nature of sensory appetite to flee sensory sorrow (*dolor*) and bodily injury. Even where the rational will is concerned, Aquinas takes over the distinction between *will as nature or functioning by way of nature*, which refuses what seems contrary to nature or bad in itself, and *will* functioning *by way of reason*, which may will some of those very things *for the sake of a good enough end*.[241] During Christ's *ante-mortem* career, these appetites were allowed to function normally,[242] insofar as this was compatible with His sinlessness and perfect virtue. Thus, Christ's sensory appetite as well as His will as nature refuse His passion and death, while His will functioning by way of reason wills them for the sake of human salvation. At the same time, His rational will functioning by way of reason was fully conformed to His Divine will,[243] and neither was obstructed by the motion of His sensory appetites or will as nature.[244]

In the same vein, Aquinas allows, Christ's human soul would experience passions and emotions insofar as these are compatible with perfect knowledge and virtue. To begin with, he offers a precise distinction between *dolor* whose object and motive is wounding caused by the sense of touch, and *tristitia* whose object is harm or evil apprehended by reason or imagination (e.g., the loss of money or grace),[245] and he assigns both to the sensory appetite. When Christ's body was cut by thorns and whips and punctured by nails and spears, He experienced sensory pain and sorrow (*dolor*).[246] Where *tristitia* is concerned, Aquinas enters an ancient philosophical controversy; for the Stoics had denied that the wise can experience it on the ground that nothing evil can happen to them. The Angelic Doctor explains this was because they had narrowed the categories of good and evil to integrity (*honestum*) and lack

thereof (*inhonestum*). Aquinas counters that while
these are important, they do not exhaust the category of human goods and ills, respectively. Christ's
human soul can experience *tristitia* insofar as He
can apprehend things harmful to Himself (e.g., His
passion and death) or to others (e.g., the sins of the
disciples or the Jews who killed Him).[247] Indeed,
tristitia is among the punishments of sin that He
assumes for our sake.[248]

Strictly speaking, because fear is caused by uncer-
tainty about future evil[249] and amazement (*admira-
tio*) involves an element of surprise,[250] each is incompatible with Christ's perfect knowledge. Aquinas
accommodates Scriptural texts about Christ's being
troubled and distressed (Mark 14:33), and being
amazed (Matthew 8:10), by saying that Christ assumes the affect that goes with these emotions without the cognitive defects.[251]

Anger might seem a more difficult emotion. After all, James 1:20 denies it can work the righteousness of God; Gregory says it blinds the mind's eye;
Aristotle insists it is incompatible with gentleness,
which Scripture attributes to Christ. Yet, in the story
of Christ's cleansing the Temple, John 2:17 quotes
Psalm 68:10: "Zeal for thy house will consume me."
Aquinas' strategy is similar to Bonaventure's when
he explains how anger is a composite emotion in-
volving both *tristitia* and a vindictive appetite, which
latter can occur with, as well as without an appropriate order to reason. Christ's perfect virtue rules
out any vindictive motive contrary to reason but
not that in accord with reason. Hence, His human
soul can experience praiseworthy anger.[252] Naturally

speaking, even reasonable anger would draw off energy from the rest of the soul's powers. In Christ's case, this doesn't happen because Divine power prevents it, allowing each power to function in its own way.[253] Again, reason can use anger as an instrument in service of justice,[254] and thus moderated, it is not incompatible with gentleness.[255]

Like Lombard and Bonaventure, Aquinas concludes that Christ in His human nature was both a pilgrim (*viator*) and a comprehender (*comprehensor*), but he gives shorter shrift to how it is metaphysically possible for Christ to straddle these two states. He explains simply that during His *ante-mortem* career, Christ lacked happiness with respect to His mortal, passible body, but He had the happiness proper to the soul insofar as He saw God plainly with His mind.[256]

5.5. Summary

Although Aquinas' account of Christ's *ante-mortem* human nature joins Bonaventure in following the main lines of Lombard's "harmony" of patristic sources—attributing to His soul fullness of knowledge and grace, beatific vision, and the virtues compatible with it; denying omnipotence; affirming a passible mortal body as well as genuine emotions fully subject to reason's control—it draws on the Angelic Doctor's metaphysics, cognitive and moral psychology to fill in philosophical details. In principle, for Aquinas, Scripture sets an upper bound on soteriological speculation: assertions should not venture beyond *explicit* Biblical claims and what clearly follows from them. In practice, Aquinas imi-

tates Church fathers in allowing his exegesis to be
affected by his philosophical commitments. Hap-
pily, where Christology is concerned, the tensions
in the latter mirror those found in the Scriptural
texts. Thus, Aquinas' image of grace—like being and
goodness—as cascading down in decreasing measure from a boundless source, presses towards maxi-
mizing the assumed nature's perfection; while his
sense that grace does not obliterate but builds on
top of nature provides incentive to "hold back"—
forces realistic attention to natural capacities and
provides incentive for preserving natural alongside
miraculous functioning. Once again, Christ's *ante-
mortem* body is said to be very much like ours, but
supernatural advantages make His soul very different from our own!

VI. Scotistic Subtleties

So far, our survey shows how philosophical considerations interact with theological *desiderata* to
produce a portrait of Christ's human nature. On
the one hand, philosophical analyses of human capacities function to set an upper bound on the
excellences that can be "loaded in." On the other,
theological commitments lead philosophy to fresh
and surprising estimates of human capacities.

With Scotus, the latter trend definitely dominates
and finds expression in his methodological rule:
where Scripture and Ecclesiastical pronouncements
underdetermine the issue, it is better to praise Christ
too much than too little.[257] This venturesome policy
in Christology contrasts with Aquinas' and moves

beyond Bonaventure's appreciation to enthusiastic sponsorship of the conclusion that God would have become Incarnate even if Adam had not fallen.

6.1. Incarnation at the Heart of Creation

For Scotus, God is a maximally well-organized lover. The persons of the Trinity love one another with friendship love (*amor amicitiae*), which is unselfish and so reaches out to desire other co-lovers for the Beloved. Accordingly, God wills to create the soul of Christ to love God in the highest degree that anything external can, and to be the Head of a vast community of created co-lovers (angelic and human) destined for the beatific intimacy of sharing in the Trinitarian love-life.[258] Hypostatic union is a way of honoring the soul of Christ, as it were "the wedding garment" that makes a creature "fit" for this role.[259] Like other rational creatures, the soul of Christ is also "suited" with infused grace, which becomes—by means of free and contingent Divinely established statutory conventions—the condition of Divine acceptance. If hypostatic union and infused grace are proximate means to the Divine end of swelling the community of co-lovers, the material world is a remote means. Because human souls are (according to Scotus' Aristotelian metaphysics) "incomplete beings," and because Divine consistency of purpose attends to the exigencies of nature, God wills to create the material world as the environment in which humans can "live and move and have their being."[260] Important for present purposes is that—on Scotus' account—all of this is "settled" prior in the order of explanation to Divine permis-

sion and fore/middle knowledge of sin. Otherwise,
the best thing God does in creation would be moti-
vated by the worst thing creatures do—which would
be irrational![261] Once sin comes into the picture,
Christ volunteers for a "secondary" mission of making satisfaction for the sin of Adam's race.[262] On this
scenario, the exigencies of Trinitarian love-life set
the dominant, perfection-maximizing tone, while
the requirements of satisfaction enter as a minor
theme requiring small variations and adjustments.

6.2. The Limited Impact of Hypostatic Union

One technical issue directly and indirectly affect-
ing Scotus' characterization of Christ's human nature centers on the metaphysical implications of
hypostatic union.[263] Everyone agrees that the assumed nature and its inherent qualities and relations are created and hence finite in themselves. All
concur that hypostatic union makes any thoughts,
volitions, and passions occurring in Christ's human
soul to be the acts of an infinite supposit (i.e., the
Divine Word). Aquinas joins Anselm and Bonaventure in assuming that hypostatic union makes the
suffering and obedience unto death ontologically
commensurate with the infinite offense of Adam's
race. Drawing on his doctrine of being (*esse*) as the
actuality of essence, Aquinas reasons that just as organic parts share in the being (*esse*) of their supposit
in such a way that a transplanted kidney would first
participate in the being (*esse*) of the donor and then
in the being (*esse*) of the recipient; so the assumed
human nature participates in the infinite being (*esse*)
of its supposit, the Divine Word. Scotus rejects

Aquinas' theory of the relation between essence and being (*esse*), insisting that each really distinct thing (*res*) has its own being (*esse*): the Divine essence is infinite being; the matter, substantial forms, inherent accidents of the assumed nature their own distinct being (*esse*). According to Scotus' metaphysical analysis, hypostatic union is simply a real relation (a *res relativa*) inhering in the nature, and relative things do nothing to alter the intrinsic character of absolute things (in this case of the substantial form of intellectual soul and the qualities—thoughts, volitions, passions—inhering in it). The *res relativa* that hypostatic union is, is metaphysically too slight to augment the active or passive causal capacities of the human nature assumed.[264] *A fortiori*, it cannot by itself change the metaphysically finite into anything metaphysically infinite.[265] Thus, Scotus rejects as incoherent because metaphysically impossible Anselm's demand for an ontologically commensurate satisfaction, and Scotus insists that God could have accepted anything He wanted.[266] Nor (*pace* Aquinas) does the choice of Christ's suffering and death as satisfactory reflect Divine severity but rather the propriety of God's best beloved creatures, imitating Divine generosity in voluntarily offering Himself on behalf of the community of human co-lovers of which He is the Head.[267]

6.3. Voluntary versus Natural Agency

Scotus' high doctrine of Divine and created freedom[268] comes into play in challenging the "Great Chain" analogies deployed by Aquinas and picked up by Henry of Ghent. The latter compare the flow of perfection into Christ's soul to *natural* causal processes. According to Scotus, God is not a natural cause of anything *ad extra*, but acts as *voluntary* agent freely and contingently in creation. Infused grace and other theological virtues are produced by the Divine will according to freely and contingently established Divine statutes. Likewise, beatific vision and enjoyment involve Divine *voluntary* agency to produce the vision[269] and created *free* agency in eliciting the act of enjoyment.[270] For Scotus, God's decisions to assume and to perfect Christ's human nature are alike free and contingent, logically independent of one another and of that soul's own freely elicited acts.

6.4. "Lower than the Angels"?

Divine election of a *human soul* as the most perfect of Its created co-lovers raises the question of its essential and accidental comparison and contrast with angels. Occasionally, Scotus hints that the essentially more excellent angelic natures would have a greater claim on Divine love apart from hypostatic union.[271] At the very least, this metaphysical differential would seem to entail both greater active power for producing and more extensional passive capacity for receiving perfections.[272] How then could the soul of Christ have grace, knowledge, or beatific enjoyment (*fruitio*) in the maximum degree possible for creatures?

Nor will it help to say that the soul's receptive capacities can be expanded beyond any angel's via a Divine infusion of habits. Fundamentally, Scotus contends, powers are essentially and *immediately* perfectible by the acts with respect to which they are in potency. Thus, intellect (will) is either essentially and immediately capable of receiving certain thoughts (volitions), or no habit will be a means of enabling it to do so.[273] Rather habits play only an efficient, not a material causal role.[274] Besides, if habits could expand subjective capacity, they would do so as much for angelic as for human natures, and so could not explain how the human soul of Christ reached a capacity equal to that of the highest angel.[275] Likewise, appeal to hypostatic union would not avail, both because real relations have no capacity to alter absolute causal capacities[276] and because if they did they could augment the naturally superior angelic powers beyond those of a human soul.

Scotus' own response is that human souls *by nature* have equal passive but lesser active capacities than the angels. His argument turns on the premiss that a subject that [a] can receive an accident that comes in degrees and [b] is not limited to a determinate degree of that accident can receive any degree of that accident. He claims that grace, beatific vision, and enjoyment pertain to intellectual natures insofar as they are images of God,[277] and hence that the qualitative forms received by humans and angels are of the same species.[278] Where heat is concerned, water and air satisfy condition [a] but not condition [b]; but human as much as angelic capacity for grace, beatific vision, and enjoyment meets both conditions [a] and [b].[279] By contrast, the active causal power of naturally superior angels is greater and so is capable of contributing more perfect acts.[280]

6.5. Maximal Grace

Since the essential receptive capacities of Christ's human soul and angels are equal, God could infuse the highest possible degree of grace into any of them, whether or not they were also hypostatically united to a Divine person.[281] The maxim to praise as much as possible makes it probable that God *did in fact* confer the maximum possible grace on Christ. *De facto* Divine soteriological policies make Christ's soul alone the Head through Whom graces come to others, and so furnish a reason for God not to confer maximal grace on any other rational creatures.[282]

6.6. Supreme Enjoyment

Given that God can infuse and the soul of Christ can receive maximal grace and maximal beatific enjoyment, and yet the soul of Christ is a less perfect efficient causal power of beatific enjoyment than an angel's is, a further question arises: can Christ's soul receive maximal enjoyment without maximal grace? Arguments to the contrary appeal to soteriological commonplaces—that infused grace is required for meritorious acts and for strengthening the soul's powers, that infused charity is required for maximal happiness.[283]

Scotus meets this query with a pair of distinctions: between what is possible in the natural order of causes versus what God can do acting alone; and between what God can do with respect to His absolute versus His ordered power (*de potentia absoluta, de potentia ordinata*). So far as absolute Divine power (i.e., God's power to do whatever is metaphysically possible) alone is concerned, an affirmative answer is easy. God can supply the efficient causal power of any creature to produce the effect all by Himself.[284]

If Aquinas' God respects the agency of the assumed nature by letting its agent intellect abstract species from phantasms, Scotus' God makes room for the agency of Christ's created will. So far as God's ordered power is concerned (i.e., what accords with the soteriological statutes He has in fact legislated), God has stipulated the created will as the first efficient cause of an act of beatific enjoyment, yet in such a way that it cannot produce the effect without the presence of infused grace as a second cause.[285] For Scotus, the tricky part is how grace perfects the created act of willing. Either they will be necessarily connected in such a way that the will as principal cause cannot act to produce its effect without infused grace as secondary cause (as if the father could not act to produce a child without the concomitant action of the mother)—in which case the will cannot be an efficient cause of enjoyment without infused grace—or they will be so related that God could supply the efficient causality of the one without taking the place of the efficient causality of the other—in which case, were God to do so, the will could be an active cause of an act of enjoyment without infused grace.[286]

6.7. Impeccability
Scotus endorses the impeccability of Christ's human will, but finds it doubly problematic.

6.7.1. Impeccability, an Enemy of Autonomy?
Philosophically, the difficulty is how to reconcile

it with Christ's human freedom. True to his own action theory, Scotus maintains that the assumed human nature of itself (*de se*) was able to sin.[287] For the human will as the only rational power is a self-determining power for opposites, not only in succession (so that it wills *A* at *t1* and does not will *A* at *t2*), but without succession (so that the will as naturally prior to its action or inaction, even while willing *A* at *t1*, retains at *t1* the capacity not to will *A* at *t1*). Moreover, the human will of itself (*de se*) possesses twin native tendencies—an affection for what is advantageous (*affectio commodi*) or good for itself (*bonum sibi*), and an affection for justice (*affectio iustitiae*) or for things considered as intrinsically valuable (*bona in se*). Thus, the human will of itself is capable of both inaction contrary to right reason (by not willing or not nilling as right reason dictates) and action contrary to right reason (willing or nilling contrary to right reason but for the sake of advantage).

If so, how does Christ's human nature become impeccable? Once again, not simply by virtue of hypostatic union, because the *res relativa* that hypostatic union is could not by itself affect the soul's essential will-power,[288] and any change in the soul's capacity produced by the "metaphysically close" Divine essence would be a voluntary rather than a natural effect. Christ's human soul is rendered impeccable the same way all the Blessed are—viz., by the fullness of glory (i.e., their happiness or beatific enjoyment of the Godhead). Unlike the rest of the heavenly company, the human soul of Christ receives this happiness at the first instant of its union (which is identical with the first instant of its existence).[289]

Yet, how can fullness of glory confer impeccability without obstructing the will's freedom? Here Scotus does not follow Anselm in saying that the Divine will's causing the human will to persevere in uprightness does not amount to coercion because they belong to the same person or supposit (= the Divine Word). On the contrary, Scotus insists, because the Trinity has one action and one will *ad extra*, and Christ's human nature of itself (*de se*) is a creature, its relation to the will of the second Divine person will be no different from its relation to the will of the others to whom it is not hypostatically united. The problem about free beatitude is the same for Christ's human soul as it is for the elect generally.

Scotus' eventual answer is disappointing because it is apparently incongruous with his own distinctive doctrine of freedom. Indeed, his reasoning seems quite close to Aquinas' in distinguishing among [i] determination by causes in the agent's "own order," [ii] determination by inferior agents (e.g., in the case of the will, by a habit), and [iii] determination by some superior agent. The first two are ruled out by the will's nature as a self-determining power for opposites (in a way that they are not excluded for canine or bovine agency). But, paralleling Aquinas, Scotus maintains that God as a superior agent can determine the will without the will's altogether losing its contingency of action. For, relative to other causes in its order and/or inferior to it, the created will remains self-determining and the effect contingent, even though the effect is not contingent in relation to the superior cause. Alternatively and less plausibly, Scotus allows, one could say that the contingency of the will in its order of causes yields absolute contingency in the effect, Divine determinism notwithstanding.[290]

6.7.2. Meritorious Beatitude?

The second, theological problem is that precisely by conferring impeccability, beatitude normally closes an agent's merit-earning career. For to be meritorious, an act has to proceed from a free agent infused with grace or charity. For most humans, the period of possible merit-earning begins at the age of reason and closes with death, because they (we) pass through this present life without benefit of beatific vision and enjoyment. But the human soul of Christ is beatified and hence impeccable from the first instant of its creation. For Scotus, the bottom-line is easy: because merit is a statutory category created by free and contingent Divine soteriological legislation, God can simply build in exceptions to allow Christ to earn merit during His earthly life, despite Divine determinism preventing Him from turning away from His supernatural end.[291] (Alternatively and less plausibly, he could have replied that Christ's *ante-mortem* choices are free because not determined by any cause of its own or of an inferior order.)

6.8. Infinite Knowledge

Scotus' treatment of Christ's human knowledge confronts at multiple levels the question of whether finite created intellects can have knowledge of the infinite. Since he is ascribing to Christ from the beginning knowledge that other blessed have *post mortem*, his discussion forces an analysis of created intellectual capacities generally and not merely of Christ's human soul as a special case.

In addition to his now-familiar distinction between an agent's passive capacity to receive and its active power to produce a given act, Scotus appropriates another distinction between *extensional* versus *intensional* infinity. God alone is intensively infinite; as essentially finite, no creature can be intensively infinite. As Bonaventure already noted, St. Augustine's claims that Christ and the Blessed see God and see all things in God raise both problems at once—about the created intellect's ability to cognize the intensively infinite and its capacity to grasp an extensional infinity. If Bonaventure argued for extensional infinity in the objects of *habits*, Scotus takes a further step when he denies that either intensive or extensional infinity in the *object* of cognition implies intensive infinity in the cognitive *act*.

(1) Where the act of seeing God is concerned, Scotus maintains that created intellects have a *passive* capacity to be *immediately* affected thereby. *Pace* Bonaventure and Henry of Ghent, *prior* absolute forms ("light") would be superfluous, because the latter are required only where the object is either not intelligible of itself (e.g., the way natural forms are not but require the agent intellect to render them intelligible) or somehow is not strong enough by itself to produce the act in the cognitive power. The Divine essence, however, is maximally intelligible and as omnipotent is the maximally perfect motive

power.[292] And in any event (as noted before), *beatific vision* is not a natural process, but requires the *voluntary* action of God. Because—in Scotus' estimate—angelic and human *receptive* capacities are equivalent, Christ's human soul can receive a vision of God that is as perfect as any creatures' can be.

(2) Seeing all things in the Word as in a mirror or exemplar can be construed in two ways, however. One way posits a single act of cognition whose principal object is the Divine Word and whose secondary objects include all possible creatures. The other distinguishes one act of seeing God from multiple acts of seeing creatures. Either way, Aquinas hesitated to say that Christ *actually* sees all *possibles,* and so an extensional infinity of creatures in the Divine Word, for the theological reason that doing so would be tantamount to *comprehending* Divine power.[293] Scotus' sparring partner Henry of Ghent focuses on the first interpretation and makes a phenomenological appeal: where human cognitive powers are concerned, the more the objects, the less obscure the cognition; therefore, infinitely many objects would mean no cognition at all! Thus, Henry claims, the soul of Christ sees everything in the Word habitually but not actually.[294]

Scotus rejects the reasoning of both. Against Aquinas, Scotus argues, the intensive infinity of the Divine essence is prior to and explains the extensional infinity of possibles shining in it. But knowing effects never furnishes *comprehensive* knowledge of a cause.[295] In fact, cognition of the effects does not even imply comprehension of the effects! Against Henry's phenomenological observation, Scotus responds that it applies at most to cognitions *actively elicited* by created intellects, but not to those *passively received*.[296] Metaphysically, an extensional infinity of objects implies an extensional infinity of relations of reason to beings of reason and so does not require intensive infinity in the really extant act.[297] In any event, those who think otherwise will have to rule out any appeal to habitual knowledge as well. For if an extensional infinity of objects implied intensive infinity in the act, so likewise in the corresponding habit.[298]

Scotus flirts with the view that the soul of Christ actually sees everything the Divine Word sees, and does so by a simultaneously inhering actual infinity of distinct cognitive acts.[299] For all intellects have being in general as their proper object, and so, for each being, are able to receive an act of understanding it. But no pair of these acts is incompossible with each other. Therefore, if there is a capacity for each and for any two, there is a *passive* capacity for receiving all simultaneously.[300] (Scotus joins many contemporaries in regularly granting such seemingly fallacious inferences from "each taken separately" to "all taken together.")

Given Scotus' doctrine that powers are naturally prior to their acts in such a way that eliciting one at a given time does not take away the power at that time for eliciting another at that time, Scotus could venture further to assign the intellect *active* power at a given time to elicit each of infinitely many cognitive acts at that time. Nevertheless, because any finite power has an adequate effect such that it cannot simultaneously cause many effects of that type, no created intellect would be able to elicit them all simultaneously.[301] On this view, then, the soul of Christ would be able to receive infinitely many acts of cognizing all possible creatures, but would lack power to elicit all of the infinitely many at once.

Attractive as Scotus finds it, he recognizes that this last position flies in the face, not only of conventional wisdom that a finite subject cannot have infinite receptive capacity, but also of the Aristotelian prohibition against a simultaneously existing actual infinity of really distinct things (*res*).[302] His alternative suggestion reverts to the more customary view that the single act through which Christ or the Blessed see the Word habituates Him or them towards knowing those that shine in the Word. Nevertheless, as finite powers they never see infinitely many simultaneously, but only some appropriate finite number.[303]

(3) St. Augustine contrasted "morning knowledge" (*cognitio matutina*) or seeing all things in the Word (their mirror or exemplar) with "evening knowledge" (*cognitio verspertina*) or seeing all things in themselves (*in genere proprio*). It was in connection with evening knowledge that Aquinas insisted that Christ's natural human cognitive powers be "reduced to act" by being loaded with supernaturally infused and naturally abstracted intelligible species of the same things. Scotus rejects such cluttering of Christ's human mind with duplicates, insisting (*pace* Aquinas) that supernaturally infused and naturally abstracted species differ, not in kind, but only with respect to their efficient causes.[304] Moreover, Aquinas' notion of "reduction to act" conflates the

issue of whether or not the created intellect actually has the cognitive acts, habits, or species inhering in it with whether or not the created intellect was a partial efficient cause of those cognitive acts. So far as the former is concerned, a full supply of supernaturally infused species suffices; as for the latter, Scotus insists, a power qua power is not the less perfect for not being exercised.[305]

Scotus' contrasting analysis of Christ's evening knowledge deploys his own evolving cognitive psychological categories and recognizes two ways in which things (common natures as well as particulars) may be known as they are in themselves: via intuitive cognition, which is of its object as *existing and present* and has its object as its real term and motive cause, or via *abstractive* cognition, which is of the same object except that it abstracts from its existence and presence and has a species as its real term and motive cause. [a] Scotus contends as above that a full complement of supernaturally infused intelligible species will suffice to give Christ's human soul habitual knowledge of all (apparently finitely many) created quiddities.[306] [b] For habitual abstractive cognition of particulars, species of common natures will not suffice, because—according to Scotus—any cluster of shareable features is itself shareable, and individuation requires positive principles that are of themselves unshareable (later so-called *"haecceities"* or "thisnesses"). Rather, species proper to each particular would be required. To assign Christ's human soul abstractive cognition of all possible creatures would mean positing a simultaneously existing actual infinity.[307] The alternatives would be to posit only a *confused* cognition of possible particulars, or to say that Christ's human soul has habitual abstractive cognition of only some possible particulars.[308] No matter which way, Scotus would limit the *actual* abstractive cognition of quiddities and singulars on the ground that finite intellects can perceive only a certain finite range simultaneously yet distinctly.[309]

[c] Where intuitive cognition is concerned, Scotus further distinguishes intuitive cognition into perfect (of objects as extant and present and caused thereby) and imperfect (of objects that were or will be extant and present, caused by means of a species that was left—in the case of memory cognitions— by perfect intuitive cognitions and that carries that information about past or future existence). The human soul of Christ never has perfect intuitive cognition of everything actual or possible, because not all such objects are extant or present at a given time.[310] Likewise, the range of memory cognitions is limited by the intuitive cognitions from which they arise.[311]

On the other hand, Scotus' argument that Christ must have some *ante-mortem* intuitive cognitions of creatures in order to know contingent propositions about their existence and disposition marks an important conceptual advance in Scotus' own cognitive psychology. Having sharpened the categories with his eye on abstractive cognition—to explain how pilgrim humans (*viatores*) and angels by their natural powers can have clear (abstractive) knowledge of the Divine essence, which nevertheless falls short of (intuitive) beatific vision—Scotus hesitated (perhaps on phenomenological grounds) to affirm that *ante-mortem* humans do have intuitive cognitions of creatures. The thrust of his argument in this passage—that it would be impossible to know contingent propositions about creatures without intuitive cognitions—combines with his anti-sceptical stance to hurtle him towards the conclusion that all pilgrim humans have intuitive cognitions as well.[312]

With reference to Luke 2:40, Scotus comments that the human soul of Christ could grow and learn with respect to such intuitive and memory cognitions,[313] but not with respect to habitual cognition of quiddities. Reverting to comparisons with the angels, Scotus treats abstractive and intuitive cognitions separately. Because abstractive cognitions have the receiving intellect and the (infused) species as their efficient partial causes, God can compensate for the greater perfection of the angelic intellects' efficient causal power by infusing Christ's human soul with more perfect species, so that Christ's abstractive cognitions are as perfect as a creature's can be.[314] By contrast, God will not be able to close the gap in the case of intuitive cognitions, because no species is involved but rather the extant and present object. Consequently, Christ's intuitive cognitions of creatures will be "a little lower" than the angels'.[315]

6.9. "Occasional" Defects

According to Scotus, God's primary purpose in Incarnation would drive towards the Divine Word's assuming a maximally perfected human nature, one in which the glory of the soul redounds to the body, thereby rendering it impassible from the beginning.[316] Nor would Christ's death be necessary for the quasi-legal reason that He deserved it as punishment for original sin or personal sin.[317] Rather Adam's fall, that eternally known but unintended side-effect of Divine purpose in creation, occasions Christ's secondary role as satisfaction-maker, a task that—by free and contingent agreement—calls for a soul that can suffer and a body that can die.[318]

6.9.1. Voluntary Mortality?

Treading well-blazed trails, Scotus affirms that Christ's death was voluntary, not violent, in the sense that He did not nill but willed to accept it, all things considered; and because freely chosen, His death was meritorious.[319] As a means to His secondary end, Christ voluntarily willed to assume a passible human nature; and it took a special miracle to prevent the soul's glory from redounding to the whole[320]

Nevertheless, the death was violent in the sense of being opposed to nature, because the soul is by nature inclined to perfect the body.[321] Scotus rejects the idea that any metaphysical necessity of dying arises from the unglorified body's being composed of matter and form (à la Aquinas) and from its including contrary qualities in different organs (as Bonaventure mentions).[322] Indeed, Scotus sounds an ecological note when he traces bodily passibility to specific *post-lapsum* contingencies. Ideally, the soul's nutritive powers would transform food to replace decaying bodily parts with new ones of equal perfection. As a consequence of the fall, weakness in the soul's powers and impurities in the food prevent the new parts from being as good as the old ones, and so inaugurate a "down-hill" trend.[323] Similarly, Christ's soul was like ours in lacking the power to preserve His body from suffering and death when cut by whips, punctured by nails, etc.[324]

More distinctive is Scotus' reflection on John 10:18 ("I have power to lay it down, and I have power to take it up again"). If the philosophers hold that human souls are infused into maximally disposed organic bodies by natural necessity, while Christians maintain that they are voluntarily infused by God in the course of embryonic development, Scotus takes it to be philosophically an open question whether or not in the resurrection the souls will not unite themselves once the bodies are appropriately reassembled.[325] If so, Christ would once again be the forerunner, pioneering each soul's future of taking its bodily life up again!

6.9.2. Sorrows like Ours?

Here Scotus frames his discussion with familiar *pro* and *contra* considerations. Scripture portrays Jesus as a "man of sorrows": "See if there is any sorrow like mine." Theology says Christ earned merit through His passion and satisfaction, both of which reside (at least partly) in the upper part of the soul. Moreover, since death is violent, the soul has a natural fear of separation from the body.[326] Yet, as Bonaventure worried, sorrow seems incompatible with the perfection already attributed to Christ's human soul. Aren't joy and sorrow (*tristitia*), vehement delight and *dolor* contraries? Are they not accompanied by contrary physiological states (dilation versus contraction)?[327] Doesn't Anselm teach that sorrow depends on the apparent occurrence of something against one's will? But Christ's impeccability means His death was voluntary because in accord with God's will.

Like Bonaventure and Aquinas, Scotus recognizes two types of sorrow—*dolor* and *tristitia*. But if Bonaventure focuses on locating *dolor* in the rational as well as the sensory faculties, and if Aquinas places both *dolor* and *tristitia* in the sensory part, Scotus assigns *tristitia* to the intellectual part alone. After a lengthy refutation of Henry of Ghent's version of the distinction, Scotus says that *dolor* results from the misfit between certain objects and the sensory powers apprehending them (e.g., certain stimuli produce a sensation of bitterness, the apprehension of which is sufficient to produce *dolor*).[328] Insofar as Christ—because of His secondary task of making satisfaction—has assumed a passible human nature in which the soul's glory does not redound to the body, Christ can certainly experience *dolor* without compromising His impeccability in any way.

As for *trisititia*, Scotus develops Anselm's intuition in a different way by distinguishing four types: [i] with respect to what is actually or habitually but *unconditionally* nilled; [ii] with respect to what is actually or habitually nilled *conditionally*; [iii] with respect to what "misfits" the will's native tendencies (viz., the *affectio commodi* and the *affectio iustitiae*); and [iv] with respect to what "misfits" sensory appetite, with which the unhabituated will has compassion to the extent that it does not will its opposite more strongly.[329] Onto this four-fold division,

Scotus maps the Augustinian distinction between the superior and lower parts of the soul, now becoming a distinction in the soul's object-focus. 'The superior part' refers strictly to the soul insofar as it is concerned only with what is eternal; broadly, to the soul insofar as it is concerned with the eternal rules and wills by reference to them.

The strict-sense superior part of the human soul cannot experience *tristitia*, because that would mean nilling God in Himself or nilling some perfection internal to Him. Not even the damned nill Divine Justice absolutely, but only conditionally, insofar as It is punishing them.[330] Taken broadly, Christ cannot experience *tristitia* with respect to His own sin, because He is impeccable, but with respect to the sins of others—e.g., the unfaithfulness of doubting disciples or the unbelief and cruelty of His persecutors.[331] Moreover, for the broad-sense superior part of Christ's soul to experience *tristitia* with respect to His passion, it is enough that it is contrary to His human will's *affectio commodi*, even if it accords with its *affectio iustitiae* and even if a greater good follows it.[332] Likewise, the will as nature, when faced with the passion, experiences *tristitia* in sympathy with the senses.[333] The broad-sense superior part of Christ's soul could nill the passion *on condition* that human prosperity and Divine justice could equally well be served. But nilling the passion, all things considered, would not conform to its norms, and so Christ's human soul could neither do this nor experience *tristitia* with respect to it.[334] Thus, Scotus embraces the Lombardian consensus that Christ's human perfection is compatible with His soul's ex-

periencing a significant range of appetitive resistance
to Divine will, short of unconditionally nilling what
God commands.

VII. Lutheran Variations

For a different configuration of the issues, I turn
briefly to Martin Luther (1483-1546), one of the
giants of the Protestant reformation. Like his medieval predecessors, Luther took his intellectual for-
mation from monastic and school theology, and was
highly familiar with not only patristic but also Aristotelian philosophical theology. Yet, the German
universities in which he studied and taught already
reflected a shift by some professors (Luther included)
away from *philosophical* towards *Biblical* theology.
The new interest in philology and the revival of ex-
pertise in Biblical languages stimulated renewed
engagement with the texts of Scripture, prompting
theologians to embrace the patristic project of wrest-
ing doctrine more directly from the Bible itself.

Luther's soteriology brings out of this treasury
things both old and new. In describing the saving
work of Christ, he concentrates on three traditional
tasks—viz., satisfying Divine justice, conquering the
devil, and charting a pattern for our *ante-mortem*
lives—but he develops them in distinctive ways.

7.1. Righteous Wrath

In Anselm's satisfaction-theory, the argument proceeds at a high level of legal abstraction: created sinners incur a debt they cannot pay. Luther sticks closer
to Biblical language (especially of Paul's epistle to

the Romans), and perhaps to his own spiritual experience, when he identifies *wrath* as a righteous God's response to sin. God the Son shows Divine love for human sinners by volunteering to become human and offer Himself as a substitute target for Divine wrath. Luther explicitly agrees, this task can be accomplished only insofar as Christ is *innocent* in His human nature—neither *is* nor *does* anything contrary to the Divine will. Otherwise He would be liable for punishments of His own.[335]

7.2. Alien Imputation

Luther describes the legal transaction involved in such penal substitution with the fresh imagery that more deeply implicates Christ in our *post-lapsum* human condition. Borrowing from his teacher Staupitz, Luther explains that Christ marries the soul with the wedding ring of faith (= an infused confidence that God will be good to you, that the promises of God are true for you). Prior to the marriage, the law evaluates the prospective bride and groom separately—renders a guilty verdict on Adam's offspring and condemns them/us to hell, while pronouncing Christ innocent and righteous. But the legal estate of marriage involves "community" property: all that is Christ's belongs to the believing soul, and vice versa. Thus, the human sinner is *justified* by God's *imputing* to him/her the righteousness of Christ, while *imputing* to Christ the soul's sin and liability to death and damnation.[336] As a result of this "joyful exchange," the sinner is dead to the whole law in the sense that it can no longer render a "guilty" verdict against him/her.[337] More remarkably, where school theologians say that Christ takes our *penalties*, Luther boldly insists that alien imputation awards Him our *guilt* and *liability* to punishment as well.

7.3. Coincidence of Opposites

Next, Luther invokes the Bonaventurian theme of the Coincidence of Opposites. If human souls are legally justified by this imputation of "alien righteousness," their psycho-spiritual condition remains in disarray, with flesh warring against the spirit. Likewise, Christ remains in a state of psycho-spiritual innocence, even when our sin and liability to punishment is legally imputed to Him. Therefore, Luther proclaims, not only the believing human but also Christ is *simul iustus et peccator*![338] Notice, these are not strictly contradictory or contrary opposites, but represent two different types or levels of evaluation—one based on the actual condition and performance of the human agency, and the other on legal contracts.

In any event, Christ does not remain *simul iustus et peccator*, and even we are slated for gradual psychospiritual improvements. At this point, the other two soteriological themes enter. Christ's psycho-spiritual innocence in both Divine and human natures combines with Divine power to raise the dead, to conquer the devil: for the tempter is allowed to do his worst, but succeeds neither in seducing Christ to disobedience nor in permanently killing Him. Likewise, Christ's cruciform *ante-mortem* career instructs us, His continuing presence empowers us daily to crucify our sinful flesh by making no concession to its desires (yet another Pauline theme).

7.4. Sighs of Dereliction

Luther's second bold departure from patristic and scholastic majority reports comes with his estimate of the penalties Christ endured on our behalf. To be "tempted as we are without sin" (Hebrews 4:15), it is not enough that Christ's body be capable of damage, His soul able to feel *dolor* and *tristitia,* His will as nature express its tendency to flee death. He must also participate in the psychological torment of apparent abandonment by God. The soul's worst *ante-mortem* hell is the horror of conscience at being accused by the law, seemingly condemned to God's eternal wrath, and being deserted by God. Rejecting patristic exegesis,[339] Luther takes Jesus' quotation on the cross—"My God, my God, why hast thou forsaken me?" (Ps.22:1; cf. Mk 15:34; Mt 27:46)—as an expression of just such dereliction[340] Although Christ's human nature was taken from the Virgin's womb pure, in no way infected by sin,[341] alien imputation placed him "under the law" (Gal 4:4) not only so that He would free us from the ceremonial law or fulfill the decalogue, but to be accused by the law and condemned by it (Gal 3:13).[342] Thus, Christ experiences the temptation to blaspheme and curse God, but comes through steadfastly loyal.[343] To the objection that the cry itself—"My God, my God, why hast thou forsaken me?..."—is a sin, Luther denies it. Even if we in the throes of temptation could not utter this cry without sin, Christ could and did because His tree was good while ours are evil.[344]

Luther's rhetoric makes him enthusiastic rather than apologetic about Pauline claims that Christ was made curse (Gal 3:3) and sin (2 Cor 5:21) for us. His exposition cashes these metaphors in terms of the following four claims: [i] our sin and liability to punishment are imputed to Christ; [ii] Christ suffers the penalties for sin; [iii] the latter include a subjective experience of being accused, condemned, and cursed by the law; and [iv] human onlookers mistake Him for a sinner.[345] Once again, Luther strides beyond Aquinas and other school theologians principally in his theory of alien imputation and his deepened estimate of the penalties involved.

Luther's rhetorical delight in the Coincidence of Opposites[346] denies us any thorough analysis of the psychological implications of the experience of dereliction. Presumably, it would be incompatible with Christ's human soul simultaneously experiencing beatific vision, seeing all things in God, etc. Nor does Luther elaborate on the innocent soul's capacity to weather horrendous temptations, which seemingly reflects a high estimate of the unfallen will's power. By contrast with school theologians, minute detailing of such consequences lies outside his purpose and style.

VIII. Concluding Observations

What sort of human nature did Christ assume? In answering this question, our medieval authors all settle down on and spread out within the boundaries of a distinctive section of the conceptual map. For they inherit a tradition in which both philosophy and theology conspire to create a presumption against Incarnation. Jewish and Moslem monotheism join Neo- and Augustinian Platonizing philosophy in so stressing the metaphysical "size-gap" between God and creatures as to make the idea that God assumes any created nature into hypostatic union appear both blasphemous and metaphysically indecent. Cast in terms of *communicatio idiomatum*, it would mean that all of the limitations that pertain to human being could be truly predicated of God! Even where the exigencies of human redemption and the Pseudo-Dionysian theme of God as Self-Diffusing Goodness are allowed to override to permit the *exitus* of the Divine Word into creation, the negative presumption reasserts itself in modified form, in the demand that the assumed nature be as deiform as possible. Such "top-down" pressure to endow Christ's humanity with maximal perfection is reinforced by the "bottom-up" thrust of soteriological considerations. The doctrine that Christ assumes something from each of the four states of human being brings with it the necessity of His human nature's being outfitted with everything required for the *reditus* of human being into the glory of beatific union with God. This splits into the demand that He be glorified (with fullness of grace, knowledge, and beatific enjoyment) from the first instant of creation, the prototype and pioneer of our eschatological destiny; and that He take on enough of our pilgrim defects to be able to demonstrate the virtues that we will need to develop for our own

return to God. Even when Scotus lets Divine generosity underwrite an "Incarnation-no-matter-what"
policy, he imagines God focussed on glory—on
"bringing many sons to glory," on sharing Trinitarian
friendship love with the soul of Christ and other
co-lovers—and on willing the conditions that suit
them for such glorious life.

At first, only soteriological considerations stand
in the way of letting the glory of beatific enjoyment
redound, from the very beginning, into every aspect of Christ's human being. All of our authors
point to satisfaction-making and merit-earning as a
reason for Christ's assuming a passible, mortal nature (Anselm and Luther add conquering the devil
to this list). Christ's suffering and struggles not only
furnish us with an inspiring model of needed virtues, but demonstrate against the heretics the reality of Christ's human nature. As we move forward
from Anselm through Lombard, Aquinas, and Scotus, the reality of Christ's human nature takes on a
more positive cast in the form of a concern to find a
normally functioning human nature underlying His
already glorified state.

For our medieval authors, the verdicts of sinlessness and impeccability are overdetermined. If the
infidels might have appealed to *communicatio
idiomatum* against any Incarnation at all, Bonaventure appeals to it only to rule out sinfulness and
peccability: because God is not, cannot be a sinner,
neither can there be any insubordinate defection of
will in the human nature God assumes. In any event,
sin is incompatible with a state of glory (*non posse
peccare*), and sin is disqualifying for other salient

soteriological offices—for making satisfaction, for earning merit, for conquering the devil, for furnishing an inspiring role model. Hebrews 4:15 specifies sinlessness, but the presumption of deiformity means that impeccability trumps.

By serving as a point of contrast, Luther exposes the assumptions behind this family of Christologies as less than self-evident. Luther rejects Lombard's intuition that it is both fitting and expedient that all stages of the human condition—from pristine beginnings, through the fall and grace, to eschatological restoration—be temporally telescoped onto every moment of Christ's this-worldly career. The Reformer does not start with metaphysical proprieties, but with Biblical reflections on Christ's saving work. "Lutheran" penal substitution requires Christ's human nature to be psychologically much more like ours, even to the point of feeling abandoned and cursed by God. Nevertheless, Luther shares with our medieval authors a commitment to the "Augustinian" view that human nature was (and so is the kind of thing that could be) created originally innocent and upright, as well as the assumption that a human being pass from infancy through childhood and still arrive at adulthood in sinless condition.

Relative to his medieval predecessors, Luther extends the way God in Christ identifies with us, beyond *metaphysical* identification in Incarnation, and *biological* identification involved in taking a human nature from Adam's race, to the *legal* identification of community property and to alien imputation of guilt and liability to punishment. But he does not even flirt with letting Galatians 3:3 or 2 Corinthians

5:21 dominate Hebrews 4:15, to recognize any actual sin in Christ's human nature, since the latter would rob Christ of the capital needed for the joyful exchange.

Prompted by the Reformer, we might take a page from one of Bonaventure's objectors to note that the metaphysical "size-gap" does not, by itself, obviously demand a deiform nature. A refined sense of Divine dignity and the metaphysical incommensuration between God and creatures could reduce even the most perfected human nature to the status of earthworms and maggots, thereby making all of the fuss—about sinless versus sinful, about which emotions of what strength, about how much knowledge of which kinds—seem ridiculous. Could not self-diffusing Goodness, superabundant generosity find a "smidgen" more scope for its extravagance by identifying itself with the messy developmental process we struggle through? From a systematic point of view, if satisfaction is optional for God (as Aquinas and Scotus believed), were it forgone, why would God's human nature need to be so innocent? What if God's soteriological task is to redeem by making even horror-filled human lives meaningful? What if God's principal strategy were to sanctify them by metaphysical identification? Wouldn't Incarnation into a human nature that not only suffers but perpetrates horrors fill that bill? Which would furnish more hope: the appearance of a God-man Whose human nature represents our lost past and promised future? or Divine identification with our present misery, God's taking human being in all of its uncleanness into hypostatic union with Godself?

All of our medieval authors were committed to the infallible truth of Holy Scripture. Yet, they inherited from the patristic period a flexible hermeneutic that enabled them to harmonize by creative interpretations that explain away. Luke 2:52 is made to stand with claims of beatific vision, the knowledge of vision, or habitual omniscience. Hebrews 2:18 and 4:15 are made compatible with impeccability and right reason's invincible control. By contrast, early twentieth century theologians were eager to read the Gospels as an historical record. Many of them preferred to establish their Christological baseline with the Synoptic career and passion narratives, and Hebrews 4:15; to make "like us except for sin" their first approximation; and to design for Christ as normal an *ante-mortem* human nature as possible given that sin must be taken away. In effect, they reversed Anselmian burdens of proof, placing the onus instead on any who wish to assign Christ's human nature special advantages or perfections that would lift Him out of the rough and tumble of our *post-lapsum* world.

What sort of human nature did Christ assume? However familiar, these medieval accounts reflect a flexible Biblical hermeneutic and the weighted interplay of distinctive theological and philosophical assumptions. Surveys of other sections of the conceptual map will have to await another paper and another day.

Marilyn McCord Adams
Yale University

Notes

1. Shorter versions of this paper were presented at the Pacific Division meeting of the Society of Christian Philosophers at Seattle Pacific University in 1996, and at a conference "The Incarnation: Medieval Perspectives" at Yale University in 1998. I am grateful for audience comments, as for the helpful feedback from my colleague Rowan Greer.

2. Cf. Peter Lombard's fourfold division in *Sent.* III, d.16,c.2; *Sententiae in IV libris distinctae* (Grottaferrata (Rome): College of St. Bonaventure at Clear Water, 1971), vol. II, p.105 [hereafter Grottaferrata II.105]: Boethius offers a three-fold division in *Liber contra Eutychen et Nestorium*, c.viii, between the state into which Adam was created, the state into which he would have entered had he not fallen, and the state into which he in fact entered upon his fall; and these perhaps reflect Augustine's division into *posse peccare/posse non peccare, non posse non peccare, non posse peccare.* Such divisions are present in various degrees of implicitness or explicitness in many patristic writers as well.

3. *Cur Deus homo* II.11; *Opera omnia ad fidem codicum recensuit.* Edited by F.S. Schmitt. (Edinburgh: Thomas Nelson & Sons, 1938-1961), vol.II, p.111, lin.8-14 [hereafter Schmitt II.111, 8-14].

4. *Cur Deus homo* II.11; Schmitt II,111,26-112,3.

5. *Cur Deus homo* II.13; Schmitt II.112,22-24.

6. *Cur Deus homo* II.8; Schmitt II.103,7-19.

7. *Cur Deus homo* II.8; Schmitt II.104,3-11.

8. *Cur Deus homo* II.10; Schmitt II.106,13-16.

9. *Cur Deus homo* II.10; Schmitt II.107,6-9.

10. *Cur Deus homo* II.13; Schmitt II.112,22-113,15.

11. *Cur Deus homo* II.1; Schmitt II.97,4- 98,5.

12. *Cur Deus homo* II.2,10-11; Schmitt II.98,7-11; II.11; Schmitt II.109.6-19.

13. *Cur Deus homo* II.11; Schmitt II.111,12-14.

14. *Cur Deus homo* II.11; Schmitt II.109,20- 110,7-5.

15. *Cur Deus homo* II.11; Schmitt II.111,29- 112,1-4.

16. *Cur Deus homo* II.11; Schmitt II.111,9-18.

17. *Cur Deus homo* II.13; Schmitt II.112,26-27.

18. *Cur Deus homo* II.12; Schmitt II.112,10-12.

19. *Sent.* III,d.15,c.1,sec.7; "Omnes igitur defectus nostros suscepit Christus praeter peccatum, quos ei conveniebat suscipere et nobis expediebat."

20. *Sent.* III,d.16,c.2; Grottaferrata II.105.

21. *Sent.* III,d.12,c.3,sec.1; Grottaferrata II.82.

22. *Sent.* III,d.12,c.3,sec.2; Grottaferrata II.82.

23. *Sent.* III,d.12,c.3,sec.3; Grottaferrata II.83.

24. Romans 5:9; cf. *Sent.* III,d.19,c.1,sec.1 & c.2; Grottaferrata II.118.

25. Romans 5:8; cf. *Sent.* III,d.19,c.1,sec.2; Grottaferrata II.118.

26. I Peter 2:24; *Sent.* III,d.19, c.4; Grottaferrata II.121-122.

27. *Sent.* III,d.18,c.5,sec.1; Grottaferrata II.116.

28. *Sent.* III,d.18,c.2,sec.1-2; Grottaferrata II.113.

29. *Sent.* III,d.13,c.u,sec.1-3; Grottaferrata II.84-85.

30. *Sent.*III,d.13,c.u,sec.4; Grottaferrata II.85.

31. *Sent.*III,d.13,c.u, secs. 6,9; Grottaferrata II.86-87.

32. *Sent.* III,d.18,c.4,sec.2; Grottaferrata II.116.

33. *Sent.* III,d.13,c.u,secs.5-6,9; Grottaferrata II.86-87.

34. *Sent.* III,d.14,c.1,sec.2; Grottaferrata II.89-90.

35. *Sent.* III,d.14,c.1,secs.3-6; Grottaferrata II.90-91.

36. *Sent.* III,d.14,c.2,sec.1; Grottaferrata II.91.

37. *Sent.* III,d.15,c.2,secs.1-3; Grottaferrata II.92-93.

38. *Sent.* III,d.14,c.2,sec.1; Grottaferrata II.91.

39. *Sent.* III,d.14,sec.3; Grottaferrata II.92.

40. *Sent.* III,d.19,c.2; Grottaferrata II.120-121.

41. *Sent.* III,d.19,cc.3-4; Grottaferrata II.118-120.

42. *Sent.* III,d.18,c.5; Grottaferrata II.116-118; cf. d.15,

c.1,sec.1; Grottaferrata II.92-93.

43. *Sent.* III,d.15,c.1,sec.11-12; Grottaferrata II.96-97.

44. *Sent.* III,d.15,c.1,sec.7; Grottaferrata II.95.

45. *Sent.* III,d.15,c.1,sec.1; Grottaferrata II.92-93.

46. *Sent.* III,d.15,c.1,secs.8-12; Grottaferrata II.95-97; cf. Isaiah 53:4; Matthew 26:38; Mark 14:33; Psalm 87:4; John 12:27; Luke 19:41; Matthew 27:35.

47. *Sent.* III,d.15,c.1,sec.7; Grottaferrata II.95.

48. *Sent.* III,d.15,c.1,sec.3; Grottaferrata II.93.

49. *Sent.* III,d.15,c.1,secs.1,5; Grottaferrata II.92-94.

50. *Sent.* III,d.15,c.1,sec.8; Grottaferrata II.95-96.

51. *Sent.* III,d.15,c.2,secs.1,3; Grottaferrata II.98-99; c.3, secs.1-2,5; Grottaferrata II.100-103.

52. *Sent.* III,d.16,c.1,secs.1-2; Grottaferrata II.103-104.

53. *Sent.* III,d.17,c.2,secs.1,3; Grottaferrata II.106-107.

54. *Sent.* III,d.15,c.1,sec.4; Grottaferrata II.93-94.

55. *Sent.* III,d.17,c.2,sec.2; Grottaferrata II.106.

56. *Sent.* III,d.15,c.2,secs.1-3; Grottaferrata II.98-99.

57. *Sent.* III,d.20,a.1,qq.2,5,6; in *Opera omnia* (Quarrachi: College of St. Bonaventure, 1887),vol.III,pp.419-422, 427-432 [hereafter Quarrachi III.419-22,427-432].

58. *Sent.* III,d.1,a.2,q.1; Quarrachi III.23, 27.

59. *Sent.* III,d.1,a.2,q.1; Quarrachi III.20; d.1,a.2,q.2; Quarrachi III.22.

60. *Sent.* III,d.1,a.2,q.2; Quarrachi III.23.

61. *Sent.* III,d.1,a.2,q.2; Quarrachi III.20,23.

62. *Sent.* III,d.1,a.2,q.2; Quarrachi III.22-23.

63. *Sent.* III,d.1,a.2,q.2; QuarrachiIII.23.

64. *Sent.* III,d.1,a.2,q.2; Quarrachi III.22.

65. *Sent.* III,d.1,a.2,q.2; Quarrachi III.23.

66. *Sent.* III,d.1,a.2,q.2; Quarrachi III.22-23.

67. *Sent.* III,d.1,a.2,q.2; Quarrachi III.24-25.

68. *Sent.* III,d.1,a.2,q.2; Quarrachi III.24-25.

69. *Sent.* III,d.1,a.2,q.2; Quarrachi III.25; see also d.2,q.1; Quarrachi III.37-38.

70. *Sent.*III,d.1,a.2,q.2, ad 2um; Quarrachi III.26.

71. *Sent.* III,d.1,a.2,q.2,ad 3um; Quarrachi III.26.

72. *Sent.* III,d.1,a.2,q.2; Quarrachi III.26.

73. *Sent.* III,d.1,a.2,q.2,ad 2um; Quarrachi III.25-26.

74. *Sent.* III,d.2,q.1; Quarrachi III.38-39; d.13,a.1,q.1; Quarrachi III.276-277.

75. *Sent.* III,d.2,q.1, sed contra (2); Quarrachi III.37.

76. *Sent.* III,d.2,q.1,c & ad 3um, 4um, 5um; Quarrachi III.37-39.

77. *Sent.* III,d.2,q.2,c; Quarrachi III.40.

78. *Sent.* III,d.14,a.1,q.1; Quarrachi III.295-296.

79. *Sent.* III,d.14,a.1,q.1: Quarrachi III.296-298.

80. *Sent.* III,d.13,a.1,q.1; Quarrachi III.277.

81. *Sent.* III,d.13,a.1,q.2, c & ad 2um & ad 3um & ad 5um; Quarrachi III.280.

82. *Sent.* III,d.13,a.1,q.2,ad 5um; Quarrachi III.280.

83. *Sent.* III,d.13,a.1,q.2,c: Quarrachi III.282.

84. *Sent.* III,d.13,a.2,q.2,c; Quarrachi III.287.

85. *Sent.* III,d.13,a.2,q.3; Quarrachi III.289.

86. *Sent.* III,d.13,a.2,q.1,c; Quarrachi III.284-285; d.13,a.2,q.3,c; Quarrachi III.289.

87. *Sent.* III,d.14,a.2,q.2,ad 9um; Quarrachi III.314,317.

88. *Sent.* III,d.14,a.2,q.1, pro-arg (3) & c & ad 1um; Quarrachi III.307-308.

89. *Sent.* III,d.14,a.2,q.1,c; Quarrachi III.308.

90. *Sent.* III,d.14,a.2,q.1,c & ad 4um; Quarrachi III.308-309; d.14,a.2,q.2,c; Quarrachi III.311.

91. *Sent.* III,d.14,a.1,q.3,c; Quarrachi III.305-306.

92. *Sent.*III,d.14,a.2,q.1; Quarrachi III.308.

93. *Sent.* III,d.14,a.2,q.2,c & ad 1um & ad 2um & ad 3um; Quarrachi III.311.

94. *Sent.* III,d.14,a.2,q.3 c; Quarrachi III.316.

95. *Sent.* III,d.14,a.1,q.2,c; Quarrachi III.300.

96. *Sent.* III,d.14,q.1,q.1, sed-contra (1)-(4); Quarrachi III.299.

97. *Sent.* III,d.14,a.1,q.2, quod-sic (4)-(6); Quarrachi III.299.

98. *Sent.* III,d.14,a.1,q.2,c; Quarrachi III.300.

99. *Sent.* III,d.14,a.1,q.2,c; Quarrachi III.300.

100. *Sent.* III,d.14,a.2,q.3; Quarrachi III.314.

101. *Sent.* III,d.14,a.2,q.3; Quarrachi III.314-315.

102. *Sent.* III,d.14,a.1,q.3,c; Quarrachi III.305-306,316.

103. *Sent.* III,d.14,a.1,q.3,c; Quarrachi III.315.

104. *Sent.* III,d.14,a.1,q.3,c & ad 1um & ad 2um & ad 3um & ad 5um & ad 7um; Quarrachi III.316-317.

105. *Sent.* III,d.14,a.1,q.3,c; Quarrachi III.315.

106. *Sent.* III,d.14,a.3,q.1,ad 5um; Quarrachi III.319-320.

107. *Sent.* III,d.14,a.3,q.1,c; Quarrachi III.319-320.

108. *Sent.* III,d.14,a.3,q.1,c; Quarrachi III.319.

109. *Sent.* III,d.14,a.3,q.1,c & ad 4um & ad 5um; Quarrachi III.322-323.

110. *Sent.* III,d.14,a.3,q.3,c & 4um; Quarrachi III.322.

111. *Sent.* III,d.14,a.3,q.12,c; Quarrachi III.322.

112. *Sent.* III,d.14,a.3,q.2,c; Quarrachi III.323.

113. *Sent.* III,d.14,a.3,q.3,c; Quarrachi III.324.

114. *Sent.* III,d.12,a.1,q.1, pro arg (1)-(4); Quarrachi III. 262.

115. *Sent.* III,d.12,a.1,q.1,c; Quarrachi III.263.

116. *Sent.* III,d.12,a.1,q.2, quod-sic (2); Quarrachi III.264.

117. *Sent.* III,d.12,a.1,q.2,pro arg (1); Quarrachi III.264.

118. *Sent.* III,d.12,a.1,q.2,pro arg (3); Quarrachi III.264.

119. *Sent.* III,d.12,a.1,q.2,c; Quarrachi III.264-265; d.12,a.2,q.1,c; Quarrachi III.266-267; cf. d.15,a.1,q.1; Quarrachi III.333.

120. *Sent.* III,d.12,a.1,q.2, ad 4um; Quarrachi III.265; d.12,a.2,q.1,c; Quarrachi III.266-267.

121. *Sent.* III,d.12,a.2,q.1, pro arg ((1), (3), & (5); Quarrachi III.267; d.12,a.2,q.2,pro arg (3); Quarrachi III.268.

122. *Sent.* III,d.12,a.2,q.1, pro arg (4); Quarrachi III.267.

123. *Sent.* III,d.12,a.2,q.2,c & ad 2um & ad 3um & ad 4um; Quarrachi III.269.

124. *Sent.* III,d.12,a.2,q.1,c; Quarrachi III.266-267.

125. *Sent.* III,d.15,a.1,q.1, pro args (1)-(4); Quaracchi III.330.

126. *Sent.* III,d.15,a.1,q.1, sed contra (2), (3), (4); Quarrachi III.330.

127. *Sent.* III,d.15,a.1,q.1,ad

2um; Quarrachi III.331; cf.
d.12,a.1,q.2,ad 2um & ad
3um; Quarrachi III.265.

128. *Sent.* III,d.15,a.1,q.1,ad
1um; Quarrachi III.331.

129. *Sent.* III,d.15,a.1,q.1,ad
4um; Quarrachi III.331.

130. *Sent.* III,d.15,a.1,q.1;
Quarrachi III.331.

131. *Sent.* III,d.15,a.1,q.1,c &
ad 3um; Quarrachi III.333.

132. *Sent.* III,d.15,a.1,q.3,c;
Quarrachi III.334-335.

133. *Sent.* III,d.15,a.1,q.3,c &
ad 5um; Quarrachi III.335;
cf. *Sent.* III,d.16,a.1,q.3,c
& ad 5um & ad 6um;
Quarrachi III.351-352.

134. *Sent.* III,d.16,a.1,q.3,c;
Quarrachi III.351.

135. *Sent.* III,d.15,a.2,q.1, c
& ad 5um & ad 6um;
Quarrachi III.337.

136. *Sent.* III,d.16,a.1,q.2,c;
Quarrachi III.366.

137. *Sent.* III,d.16,a.1,q.3,
con-args (1), (3), (6);
Quarrachi III.368.

138. *Sent.* III,d.17,q.1,q.1,c
& ad 4um; Quarrachi
III.365.

139. *Sent.* III,d.16,a.2,q.1;
Quarrachi III.354.

140. *Sent.* III,d.16,q.2,q.1,ad
5um; Quarrachi III.355;
d.16,a.2,q.3,c & ad 4um &
ad 5um & ad 6um; Quarrachi
III.368-370.

141. *Sent.* III,d.16,a.2,q.1,ad
5um; Quarrachi II.355.

142. *Sent.* III,d.15,a.2,q.2,c;
Quarrachi III.338-339;
d.15,a.2,q.3,c; Quarrachi
III.340.

143. *Sent.* III,d.16,a.1,q.1,c &
ad 5um; Quarrachi III.347.

144. *Sent.* III,d.16,a.2,q.3;
Quarrachi III.358.

145. *Sent.*III,d.16,a.1,q.1,c;
Quarrachi III.346.

146. *Sent.* III,d.16,a.1,q.2,c &
pro-args (3) & (4);
Quarrachi III.348-349.

147. *Sent.* III,d.16,a.2,q.1;
Quarrachi III.354;
d.16,a.2, q.2, c & ad 6um;
Quarrachi III.355-357.

148. *Sent.* III,d.16,a.1,q.1,c;
Quarrachi III.354.

149. *Sent.* III,d.16,a.2,q.3,c;
Quarrachi III.359.

150. *Sent.* III,d.16,a.2,q.3,c;
Quarrachi III.358.

151. *Sent.* III,d.16,a.2,q.2,c &
con-args (2), (4), & (5);
Quarrachi III.355-356.

152. *Sent.* III,d.16,a.2,q.2,c;
Quarrachi III.356.

153. *Sent.* III,d.16,a.2,q.2,c;
Quarrachi III.356.

154. *Sent.* III,d.16,q.2,ad 5um;
Quarrachi III.357.

155. *Sent.* III,d.16,a.2,q.2,c;
Quarrachi III.356.

156. This reasoning is particularly evident in Aquinas' argument for the existence of angels in *Summa theologiæ* I,q.50,a.1.

157. *Summa theologiæ* III, q.1,a.1,c.

158. *Summa contra Gentiles* IV,c.55,sec.5.

159. *Summa theologiæ* III, q.1,a.3,c.

160. *Summa theologiæ* III, q.1,a.3,c.

161. *Summa theologiæ* III, q.1,a.3,ad 2um & ad 3um.

162. *Summa theologiæ* III, q.1,a.3,c.

163. *Summa theologiæ* III, q.1,a.3,ad 1um.

164. *Summa theologiæ* III, q.9,a.1,c.

165. *Summa theologiæ* III, q.7,a.12,c.

166. *Summa theologiæ* III, q.7,a.13,c.

167. *Summa theologiæ* III, q.8,a.1,c.

168. *Summa theologiæ* III, q.7,a.13,c.

169. *Summa theologiæ* III, q.7,a.1,c; q.8,a.1,c; cf. a.5,c; a.6,c.

170. *Summa theologiæ* III, q.8,a.3,c; cf. a.4, ad 1um.

171. *Summa theologiæ* III, q.8,a.6,c.

172. *Summa theologiæ* III, q.10,a.4,c & ad 3um.

173. *Summa theologiæ* III, q.9,a.2,c; q.10,a.1,ad 1um.

174. *Summa theologiæ* III, q.10,a.1,c.

175. *Summa theologiæ* III, q.10,a.1,ad 2um.

176. *Summa theologiæ* III, q.10,a.2,ad 3um.

177. *Summa theologiæ* III, q.10,a.2,ad 2um.

178. *Summa theologiæ* III, q.10,a.2,c & ad 2um.

179. *Summa theologiæ* III, q.10,a.2,c; cf.q.11,a.5,ad 1um.

180. *Summa theologiæ* III, q.10,a.2,c & ad 2um.

181. *Summa theologiæ* III, q.9,a.3,c.

182. *Summa theologiæ* III, q.9,a.3,c & ad 1um & ad 3um.

183. *Summa theologiæ* III, q.9,a.3,c; a.4,c; q.11,a.5,ad 1um.

184. *Summa theologiæ* III, q.11,a.1,c.

185. Cf. *Summa theologiæ* III, q.11,a.1,obj.1.

186. *Summa theologiæ* III, q.11,a.1,obj.2; a.2,objs.1-3.

187. *Summa theologiæ* III, q.11,a.1,ad 2um; a.2, c & ad 1um & 2um. For a fuller discussion of these issues, see my "The Resurrection of the Body according to Three Medieval Aristotelians: Thomas Aquinas, John Duns Scotus, William Ockham," *Philosophical Topics*, vol.20 (1992), 1-33.

188. *Summa theologiæ* III, q.11,a.2,c.

189. *Summa theologiæ* III, q.11,a.2,c & ad 2um.

190. *Summa theologiæ* III, q.9,a.4,c & ad 2um; q.12, a.2,c.

191. *Summa theologiæ* III, q.11,a.5,ad 2um.

192. *Summa theologiæ* III, q.9,a.4,ad 3um.

193. Cf. Hebrews 2:9; *Summa theologiæ* III, q.11,a.4,obj.4 & c.

194. *Summa theologiæ* III, q.11,a.4,c; a.6,ad 1um.

195. *Summa theologiæ* III, q.12,a.2,c.

196. *Summa theologiæ* III, q.12,a.3,c.

197. *Summa theologiæ* III, q.12,a.4,c.

198. *Summa theologiæ* III, q.13,a.1,c.

199. *Summa theologiæ* III, q.13,a.1,ad 2um, or to annihilate (*Summa theologiæ* III, q.13,a.2,c.)

200. *Summa theologiæ* III, q.13, a.2,obj.2.

201. *Summa theologiæ* III, q.13, a.2,obj.1.

202. *Summa theologiæ* III, q.13, a.2,obj.3.

203. *Summa theologiæ* III, q.13, a.2,c.

204. *Summa theologiæ* III, q.13,a.2,c; a.3,c.

205. *Summa theologiæ* III, q.13,a.3,obj.2.

206. *Summa theologiæ* III, q.13,a.3,c.

207. *Summa theologiæ* III, q.13,a.3,ad 2um.

208. *Summa theologiæ* III, q.13,a.3,c.

209. *Summa theologiæ* III, q.14,a.1,c.

210. *Summa theologiæ* III, q.14,a.4,ad 2um & c.

211. *Summa theologiæ* III, q.1,a.2,c.

212. *Summa theologiæ* III, q.1,a.2,c; q.46,a.1,ad 3um & a.2,ad 3um.

213. *Summa theologiæ* III, q.46,a.2,c.

214. *Summa theologiæ* III, q.14,a.1,ad 1um; a.4, c & ad 2um.

215. *Summa theologiæ* III, q.14,a.1,c & ad 1um.

216. *Summa theologiæ* III, q.14,a.4,c.

217. *Summa theologiæ* III, q.14,a.4,c

218. *Summa theologiæ* III, q.14,a.4,c.

219. *Summa theologiæ* III, q.14,a.1,ad 4um.

220. *Summa theologiæ* III, q.14,a.4,c.

221. *Summa theologiæ* III, q.14,a.1,ad 2um.

222. *Summa theologiæ* III, q.14,a.3,c; a.4,c; cf. q.15, a.5,ad 2um.

223. *Summa theologiæ* III, q.14,a.2,c.

224. *Summa theologiæ* III, q.15,a.1,c.

225. *Summa theologiæ* III, q.15,a.1,obj.1.

226. *Summa theologiæ* III, q.15,a.1,ad 1um.

227. *Summa theologiæ* III, q.15,a.1,ad 3um.

228. *Summa theologiæ* III, q.15,a.1,obj.4.

229. *Summa theologiæ* III, q.15,a.1,ad 4um.

230. *Summa theologiæ* III, q.15,a.1,ad 4um.

231. *Commentary on Saint Paul's Epistle on the Galations by St. Thomas Aquinas.* Translated by F.R. Larcher,OP (Albany, NY: Magi Books,1966), Lecture 5,chapter 3,p.86.

232. *Galatians-Commentary,* Lecture 5,chapter 3,p.87.

233. *Galatians-Commentary,* Lecture 5, ch.3,pp.87-88.

234. *Summa theologiæ* III, q.46,a.4,obj.3.

235. *Summa theologiæ* III, q.15,a.1,c.

236. *Summa theologiæ* III, q.15,a.4,c.

237. *Summa theologiæ* III, q.15,a.2,c.

238. *Summa theologiæ* III, q.15,a.2,c & ad 1um; q.27, a.3,c.

239. *Summa theologiæ* III, q.15,a.2,ad 3um.

240. *Summa theologiæ* III, q.18,a.6,ad 3um.

241. *Summa theologiæ* III, q.18,a.5,c.

242. *Summa theologiæ* III, q.18,a.5,c; a.6,c.

243. *Summa theologiæ* III, q.18,a.5,c; a.6,c.

244. *Summa theologiæ* III, q.15,a.2,ad 2um; q.18,a.6,c.

245. *Summa theologiæ* III, q.15,a.6,c; cf. *Summa theologiæ* I-II, q.35,aa.2-7.

246. *Summa theologiæ* III, q.18,a.5,c.

247. *Summa theologiæ* III, q.15,a.6,c & ad 2um.

248. *Summa theologiæ* III, q.15,a.6,ad 3um & ad 4um.

249. *Summa theologiæ* III, q.15,a.7,c; q.8,ad 1um.

250. *Summa theologiæ* III, q.15,a.8,c.

251. *Summa theologiæ* III, q.15,a.7,c; a.8,c.

252. *Summa theologiæ* III, q.15,a.9,c.

253. *Summa Theologica* III, q.15,a.9,ad 3um.

254. *Summa theologiæ* III, q.15,a.9,ad 1um.

255. *Summa theologiæ* III, q.15,a.9,ad 2um.

256. *Summa theologiæ* III, q.15,a.10,c.

257. *Op.Ox.*III,d.13,q.2; in *J. Duns Scotus: Opus Omnia* (Lyon: Laurence Durand, 1639; reprinted Hildesheim: Georg Olms Verlag, 1968), vol. VII. 1 p. 268 [hereafter Wadding VII.1, 268].

258. Duns Scotus, *Theologiae Marianae elementa.* Edited by Carolus Balic, OFM. (Kacic, 1933); hereafter = CB. *Op.Ox.*III,d.7,q.4;

CB,14-15; *Op.Ox.*III.d.13,q.4,n.8; Wadding VII.1,267.

259. *Op.Ox.*III,d.7,q.4; CB,12.

260. *Op.Ox.*IV,d.46,q.1,n.9; Wadding-Vives XX,425-426.

261. *Rep.Bar.*III,d.7,q.3; CB, 182; *Lect.Completa* III, d.7, q.3; CB,188; *Op.Ox.*III, d.7, q.4; CB,14-15.

262. *Op.Ox.*III,d.20, q. u., n.10; Wadding VII.1,430; cf. d.19, q. u., n.6; Wadding VII.1,415.

263. For a more extended discussion of this topic, see my "The Metaphysics of the Incarnation in Some Fourteenth Century Franciscans," in *Essays Honoring Allan B. Wolter* (Franciscan Institute Publications, 1985), 21-57.

264. *Op.Ox.*III,d.13,q.1,n.10; Wadding VII.1,269.

265. *Op.Ox.*III,d.20,q.u,n.8; Wadding VII.1,429; *Op.Ox.* III, d.19, q.u,nn.4,7; Wadding VII.1,413,418;

266. *Op.Ox.*III,d.20,q.u,nn.8-9; Wadding VII.1,429.

267. *Op.Ox.*III,d.20,q.u,n.10; Wadding VII.1,430.

268. For an analysis of Scotus on the will, see Allan B. Wolter, "The Native Freedom of the Will as a Key to the Ethics of Scotus," "Duns Scotus on the Will as Rational Potency," and "Duns Scotus on Will and Morality," in *The Philosophical Theology of John Duns Scotus*, edited by Marilyn McCord Adams (Cornell University Press, 1990), chapters 7-9, pp. 148-206. See also John Boler, "The Moral Psychology of Duns Scotus: Some Preliminary Questions," *Franciscan Studies,* Vol.50 (XXVIII, 1990), 31-56; "An Image for the Unity of Will in Duns Scotus," *Journal of the History of Philosophy,* Vol. 32 (1994), 23-44. Cf. Marilyn McCord Adams, "Duns Scotus on the Will as Rational Potency," *Via Scoti: Methodologica ad mentem Joannis Duns Scoti.* Edited by Leonardo Sileo. (Roma: PAA-Edizioni Antonianum, 1995), 839-854.

269. *Op.Ox.*IV,d.49,q.6,n.9; Wadding X,433.

270. *Op.Ox.*III,d.13,q.4,n.20; Wadding VII.1,276; *Op.Ox.* IV,d.49,1.6,n.9; Wadding X,433.

271. *Op.Ox.*III,d.7,q.3; CB,8.

272. *Op.Ox.* III,d.13,q.1, *pro et contra*; Wadding VII.1,258; q.2,n.1; Wadding VII.1,259.

273. *Op.Ox.*III,d.14,q.1,nn.2-3; Wadding VII.1,285-286.

274. *Op.Ox.*III,d.14,q.1,n.2; Wadding VII.1,285.

275. *Op.Ox.*III,d.14,q.1,n.2; Wadding VII.1,285.

276. As above; cf. *Op.Ox.* III,d.13,q.1,n.10; Wadding VII.1,269.

277. *Op.Ox.*III,d.13,q.1,n.3; Wadding VII.1,259; *ibid.* n.6; Wadding VII.1,266-267.

278. *Op.Ox.*III,d.13,q.1,n.5; Wadding VII.1,266-267; cf. d.13,q.3,n.18; Wadding VII.1,275.

279. *Op.Ox.*III,d.13,q.1,n.5; Wadding VII.1,266; q.2, n.15; Wadding VII.1, 272; q.3,n.18; Wadding VII.1, 275.

280. *Op.Ox.*III,d.13,q.3,n.1; Wadding VII.1,260; with Scotus' reply at *ibid.,*n.18; Wadding VII.1,275.

281. *Op. Ox.* III,d.13,q.1,n.8; Wadding VII.1,267.

282. *Op. Ox.* III,d.13,q.1,n.8; Wadding VII.1,267.

283. *Op. Ox.* III,d.13,q.4,n.1; Wadding VII.1,261.

284. *Op. Ox.* III,d.13,q.4,n.19; Wadding VII.1,275.

285. *Op. Ox.* III,d.13,q.4,n.19; Wadding VII.1,276.

286. *Op. Ox.* III,d.13,q.4; Wadding VII.1,275-276.

287. *Op. Ox.* III,d.12,q.u,n.3; Wadding VII.1,255.

288. *Op. Ox.* III,d.12,q.u,n.2; Wadding VII.1,254.

289. *Op. Ox.* III,d.12,q.u,n.2; Wadding VII.1,254.

290. *Op. Ox.* IV,d.49,q.6,n.15; Wadding X,457-458.

291. *Op. Ox.* III,d.12,q.u,n.2; Wadding VII.1,254.

292. *Op. Ox.* III,d.14,qq.1-2,n.3; Wadding VII.1,285-286.

293. *Op. Ox.* III,d.14,q.2,n.9; Wadding VII.1,292.

294. *Op. Ox.* III,d.14,q.2,n.13; Wadding VII.1,294-295.

295. *Op. Ox.* III,d.14,q.2, nn.10-11; Wadding VII.1,292-293.

296. *Op. Ox.* III,d.14,q.2,n.21; Wadding VII.1,300.

297. *Op. Ox.* III,d.14,q.2,nn. 14-15,18; Wadding VII.1, 295,298.

298. *Op. Ox.* III,d.14,q.2,n.14; Wadding VII.1,295.

299. *Op. Ox.* III,d.14,q.2, nn. 16-18; Wadding VII.1, 297-298.

300. *Op. Ox.* III,d.14,q.2, nn. 16-17; Wadding VII.1, 297.

301. *Op. Ox.* III,d.14,q.2,n.19; Wadding VII.1,298-299.

302. *Op. Ox.* III,d.14,q.2,n.18; Wadding VII.1,298.

303. *Op. Ox.* III,d.14,q.2,n.20; Wadding VII.1,299.

304. *Op. Ox.* III,d.14,q.3,nn.2-3; Wadding VII.1,302.

305. *Op. Ox.* III,d.14,q.3,n.3; Wadding VII.1,302.

306. *Op. Ox.* III,d.14,q.3,n.4; Wadding VII.1,303.

307. *Op. Ox.* III,d.14,q.3,n.5; Wadding VII.1,303-304.

308. *Op. Ox.* III,d.14,q.3,n.5; Wadding VII.1,304.

309. *Op. Ox.* III,d.14,q.3,n.5; Wadding VII.1,304.

310. *Op. Ox.* III,d.14,q.3,nn.6-7; Wadding VII.1,305-306.

311. *Op. Ox.* III,d.14,q.3,n.7; Wadding VII.1,306.

312. For fuller discussions of these developments, see

Allan B. Wolter, "Duns Scotus on Intuition, Memory, and Our Knowledge of Individuals," *The Philosophical Theology of John Duns Scotus*, edited by Marilyn McCord Adams (Ithaca, New York: Cornell Univesity Press, 1990), chapter 5, pp. 98-122. See also Stephen D. Dumont, "Theology as a Science and Duns Scotus's Distinction between Intuitive and Abstractive Cognition," *Speculum*, Vol. 64 (1989), 579-599.

313. *Op.Ox.*III,d.14,q.3,n.7; Wadding VII.1,306.

314. *Op.Ox.*III,d.14,q.4,n.1; Wadding VII.1,309.

315. *Op.Ox.*III,d.14,q.4,n.2; Wadding VII.1,309.

316. *Rep.Val.*III,d.6,q.5; CB 177-8; *Rep.Bar.*III,d.7,q.3; CB 185; *Lectura completa* III,d.7,q.3; CB 188.

317. *Op.Ox.* III, d.16, q.1, nn.5,9; Wadding VII.1, 365, 369.

318. *Op.Ox.*III,d.7,q.4; CB 15.

319. *Op.Ox.*III,d.16,q.2,n.14; Wadding VII.1,372..

320. *Op.Ox.* III,d.16, q.1, nn.5,7; Wadding VII.1, 365-367.

321. *Op.Ox.*III,d.16,q.2,n.14; Wadding VII.1,372.

322. *Op.Ox.*III,d.16,q.1,nn.3-4; Wadding VII.1,364.

323. *Op.Ox.* III,d.16, q.1, nn.6,8; Wadding VII.1, 366, 368.

324. *Op.Ox.*III,d.16,q.2,n.12; Wadding VII.1,372.

325. *Op.Ox.*III,d.16,q.2,n.13; Wadding VII.1, 372. For further discussion of these issues, see my "The Resurrection of the Body," pp. 1-33.

326. *Op.Ox.*III,d.14,q.u,n.2; Wadding VII.1,327.

327. *Op.Ox.*III,d.15,q.u,n.1; Wadding VII.1,326-327.

328. *Op.Ox.*III,d.15, q.u, n.6; Wadding VII.1,330.

329. *Op.Ox.*III,d.15, q.u, nn.15-17; Wadding VII.1,339-341.

330. *Op.Ox.*III,d.15,q.u,n.20; Wadding VII.1,344.

331. *Op.Ox.*III,d.15,q.u,n.21; Wadding VII.1,344.

332. *Op.Ox.*III,d.15,q.u,n.24; Wadding VII.1,348.

333. *Op.Ox.*III,d.15,q.u,n.26; Wadding VII.1,349.

334. *Op.Ox.*III,d.15,q.u,n.25;
Wadding VII.1,349.

335. "Psalmus Vicesimus
Primus, Hebraeis XXII."
*Operationes in Psalmos.
1519-1521*, in *D. Martin
Luthers Werke: kritische
Gesamtausgabe* (Weimar:
H. Böhlau, 1883), vol. 5,
p. 603 [hereafter WA 5,
603].

336. *On the Freedom of a
Christian* in *Martin Luther:
Selections from his Writings*,
ed. by John Dillenberger
(Garden City, N.Y.: An-
chor-Doubleday, 1961)
[hereafter = MLJD], p. 61;
Two Kinds of Righteousness.
MLJD, pp. 87-88;
Pref.Rom. MLJD, pp. 23;
Ps XXI/22; WA 5,608.

337. *On the Freedom of a
Christian* MLJD, pp. 109-
110, 113, 116.

338. *Pref.Rom.* MLJD, pp.
23,29; *Gal.Com.* MLJD,
pp. 130-133; cf. *Two Kinds
of Righteousness.* MLJD, pp.
87-88; *Ps XXI/22;* WA
5,208.

339. *Ps XXI/22*; WA 5,610.

340. *Ps XXI/22* WA 5, 601,
603-633.

341. *Ps XXI/22;* WA 5,604,
614,625.

342. *Ps XXI/22;* WA 5,603-5.

343. *Ps XXI/22*; WA 5,610-
612-613.

344. *Ps XXI/22;* WA 5,604-
605.

345. *Ps XXI/22*; WA 5,603-
604,614-615,617.

346. E.g., *Ps XXI/22*; WA
5,602.

The Aquinas Lectures
Published by the Marquette University Press
Milwaukee WI 53201-1881 USA
Volumes marked * are avaiable as e-books. See web page.

12. *History of Philosophy and Philosophical Education.*
Étienne Gilson (1947) 0-87462-112-7

13. *The Natural Desire for God.* William R.O'Connor
(1948) 0-87462-113-5

14. *St. Thomas and the World State.* Robert M. Hutchins
(1949) 0-87462-114-3

15. *Method in Metaphysics.* Robert J. Henle, S.J. (1950)
0-87462-115-1

16. *Wisdom and Love in St. Thomas Aquinas.* Étienne Gilson
(1951) 0-87462-116-X

17. *The Good in Existential Metaphysics.* Elizabeth G. Salmon
(1952) 0-87462-117-8

18. *St. Thomas and the Object of Geometry.* Vincent E. Smith
(1953) 0-87462-118-6

19. *Realism And Nominalism Revisted.* Henry Veatch (1954)
0-87462-119-4

20. *Imprudence in St. Thomas Aquinas.* Charles J. O'Neil
(1955) 0-87462-120-8

21. *The Truth That Frees.* Gerard Smith, S.J. (1956)
0-87462-121-6

22. *St. Thomas and the Future of Metaphysics.* Joseph Owens,
C.Ss.R. (1957) 0-87462-122-4

23. *Thomas and the Physics of 1958: A Confrontation.* Henry
Margenau (1958) 0-87462-123-2

24. *Metaphysics and Ideology.* Wm. Oliver Martin (1959)
0-87462-124-0

25. *Language, Truth and Poetry.* Victor M. Hamm (1960)
    0-87462-125-9

26. *Metaphysics and Historicity.* Emil L. Fackenheim (1961)
    0-87462-126-7

27. *The Lure of Wisdom.* James D. Collins (1962)
    0-87462-127-5

28. *Religion and Art.* Paul Weiss (1963) 0-87462-128-3

29. *St. Thomas and Philosophy.* Anton C. Pegis (1964)
    0-87462-129-1

30. *The University in Process.* John O. Riedl (1965)
    0-87462-130-5

31. *The Pragmatic Meaning of God.* Robert O. Johann
    (1966) 0-87462-131-3

32. *Religion and Empiricism.* John E. Smith (1967)
    0-87462-132-1

33. *The Subject.* Bernard Lonergan, S.J. (1968)
    0-87462-133-X

34. *Beyond Trinity.* Bernard J. Cooke (1969) 0-87462-134-8

35. *Ideas and Concepts.* Julius R. Weinberg (1970)
    0-87462-135-6

36. *Reason and Faith Revisited.* Francis H. Parker (1971)
    0-87462-136-4

37. *Psyche and Cerebrum.* John N. Findlay (1972)
    0-87462-137-2

38. *The Problem of the Criterion.* Roderick M. Chisholm
    (1973) 0-87462-138-0

39. *Man as Infinite Spirit.* James H. Robb (1974)
0-87462-139-9

40. *Aquinas to Whitehead: Seven Centuries of Metaphysics of Religion.* Charles Hartshorne (1976) 0-87462-141-0

41. *The Problem of Evil.* Errol E. Harris (1977)
0-87462-142-9

42. *The Catholic University and the Faith.* Francis C. Wade, S.J. (1978) 0-87462-143-7

43. *St. Thomas and Historicity.* Armand J. Maurer, C.S.B. (1979) 0-87462-144-5

44. *Does God Have a Nature?* Alvin Plantinga (1980)
0-87462-145-3

45. *Rhyme and Reason: St. Thomas and Modes of Discourse.* Ralph Mcinerny (1981) 0-87462-148-8

46. *The Gift: Creation.* Kenneth L. Schmitz (1982)
0-87462-149-6

47. *How Philosophy Begins.* Beatrice H. Zedler (1983)
0-87462-151-8

48. *The Reality of the Historical Past.* Paul Ricoeur (1984)
0-87462-152-6

49. *Human Ends and Human Actions: An Exploration in St. Thomas' Treatment.* Alan Donagan (1985) 0-87462-153-4

50. *Imagination and Metaphysics in St. Augustine.* Robert O'Connell, S.J. (1986) 0-87462-227-1

51. *Expectations of Immortality in Late Antiquity.* Hilary A Armstrong (1987) 0-87462-154-2

52. *The Self.* Anthony Kenny (1988) 0-87462-155-0

53. *The Nature of Philosophical Inquiry.*Quentin Lauer, S.J. (1989) 0-87562-156-9

54. *First Principles, Final Ends and Contemporary Philosophical Issues.* Alasdair MacIntyre (1990) 0-87462-157-7

55. *Descartes among the Scholastics.* Marjorie Greene (1991) 0-87462-158-5

56. *The Inference That Makes Science.*Ernan McMullin (1992) 0-87462-159-3

57. *Person and Being.* W. Norris Clarke, S.J. (1993) 0-87462-160-7

58. *Metaphysics and Culture.* Louis Dupré (1994) 0-87462-161-5

59.* *Mediæval Reactions to the Encounters between Faith and Reason.* John F. Wippel (1995) 0-87462-162-3

60.* *Paradoxes of Time in Saint Augustine.* Roland J. Teske, S.J. (1996) 0-87462-163-1

61.* *Simplicity As Evidence of Truth.* Richard Swinburne (1997) 0-87462-164-X

62. *Science, Religion and Authority: Lessons from the Galileo Affair.* Richard J. Blackwell. (1998) 0-87462-165-8

63.* *What Sort of Human Nature? Medieval Philosophy and the Systematics of Christology.* Marilyn McCord Adams. (1999) 0-87462-166-6

About the Aquinas Lecture Series

The Annual St. Thomas Aquinas Lecture Series began at Marquette University in the Spring of 1937. Ideal for classroom use, library additions, or private collections, the Aquinas Lecture Series has received international acceptance by scholars, universities, and libraries. Hardbound in maroon cloth with gold stamped covers. Uniform style and price ($15 each). Some reprints with soft covers. Complete set (60 Titles) (ISBN 0-87462-150-X) receives a 40% discount. New standing orders receive a 30% discount. Regular reprinting keeps all volumes available. Ordering information (purchase orders, checks, and major credit cards accepted):

Bookmasters Distribution Services
1444 U.S. Route 42
P.O. Box 388
Ashland OH 44805
    Order Toll-Free (800) 247-6553
    FAX: (419) 281 6883

Editorial Address:
Dr. Andrew Tallon, Director
Marquette University Press
Box 1881
Milwaukee WI 53201-1881
Tel: (414) 288-7298 FAX: (414) 288-3300
email: andrew.tallon@marquette.edu.

http://www.mu.edu/mupress/

ISBN 0-87462-166-6